PRACT
GOUR

Company's Coming ®

Appetizers for Entertaining

Jean Paré • James Darcy

Library and Archives Canada Cataloguing in Publication

Paré, Jean, author
    Appetizers for entertaining / Jean Paré.

Includes index.
Co-published by: Company's Coming.
ISBN 978-1-988133-00-3 (wire-o)

    1. Appetizers. 2. Cookbooks. I. Title.

TX740.P34178 2016   641.81'2   C2016-903450-X

Distributed by
Canada Book Distributors - Booklogic
11414-119 Street
Edmonton. Alberta, Canada T5G 2X6
Tel: 1-800-661-9017

We acknowledge the [financial] support of the Government of Canada.

Funded by the Government of Canada | Canadä
Finance par le gouvernement du Canada

PC: 28

TABLE OF CONTENTS

Practical Gourmet

Good company and great food create a powerful combination. When laughter and conversation mix with the heady fragrance and flavours of delicious fare, we are not just sharing a meal, we are nourishing our lives. Artfully prepared dishes awaken the senses and please the palate. And here's the secret: It can all be so simple!

Practical Gourmet is delighted to partner with Company's Coming to introduce a new series designed to help home cooks create no-fuss, sumptuous food. It is possible to wow both the eye and the palate using readily available ingredients and minimal effort. **Practical Gourmet** offers sophisticated recipes without the hassle of complicated methods, special equipment or obscure ingredients. Cook because you want to, the way you want to.

Titles in this series feature full-page colour photos of every recipe, sidebars on preparation tips and tricks, how-to photos, imaginative presentation ideas and helpful entertaining information to allow you and your guests to really savour the food…and your time together.

In the following eight chapters, great care and attention have been given to combinations of flavour, texture and presentation so that you and your guests can explore great culinary possibilities, one delicious mouthful after another.

Guests will appreciate your thoughtfulness and skill, while you revel in how easy it was to prepare these impressive morsels. With these recipes, you can cook and entertain in a relaxed atmosphere…and have fun doing it.

Approachable recipes, fabulous results, wonderful get-togethers. It all starts with *Appetizers for Entertaining*.

The Jean Paré Story

Jean Paré (pronounced "jeen PAIR-ee") grew up understanding that the combination of family, friends and home cooking is the best recipe for a good life. When Jean left home, she took with her a love of cooking, many family recipes and an intriguing desire to read cookbooks as if they were novels!

When her four children had all reached school age, Jean volunteered to cater the 50th anniversary celebration of the Vermilion School of Agriculture, now Lakeland College, in Alberta, Canada. Working from her home, Jean prepared a dinner for more than 1,000 people and from there launched a flourishing catering operation that continued for more than 18 years.

As requests for her recipes increased, Jean was often asked, "Why don't you write a cookbook?" The release of 150 Delicious Squares on April 14, 1981, marked the debut of what would soon turn into one of the world's most popular cookbook series.

"Never share a recipe you wouldn't use yourself."

Company's Coming cookbooks are distributed in Canada, the United States, Australia and other world markets. Bestsellers many times over in English, Company's Coming cookbooks have also been published in French and Spanish.

Familiar and trusted in home kitchens around the world, Company's Coming cookbooks are offered in a variety of formats. Highly regarded as kitchen workbooks, the softcover Original Series, with its lay-flat plastic comb binding, is still a favourite among home cooks.

Jean Paré's approach to cooking has always called for quick and easy recipes using everyday ingredients. That view served her well, and the tradition continues in the Practical Gourmet series.

Jean's Golden Rule of Cooking is: Never share a recipe you wouldn't use yourself. It's an approach that has worked—millions of times over!

Spiced Jam with Roasted Garlic and Cambozola

Zippy jam is partnered with robust garlic and bold Cambozola to create a tantalizing tango of tastes and textures.

Olive oil	1 tsp.	5 mL
Chopped onion	1/2 cup	125 mL
Garlic clove, minced	1	1
Ginger marmalade	3 tbsp.	45 mL
Tomato paste	2 tbsp.	30 mL
Chili paste (sambal oelek)	3/4 tsp.	4 mL
Ground cinnamon	1/4 tsp.	1 mL
Ground cumin	1/4 tsp.	1 mL
Garlic bulbs, roasted (see How To, below)	2	2
Long baguette bread slices, toasted	8	8
Cambozola cheese	4 oz.	113 g

Heat olive oil in a frying pan on medium. Add onion and garlic and cook for about 5 minutes until onion is softened.

Add next 5 ingredients and stir until heated through. Transfer to a serving bowl.

Arrange remaining 3 ingredients on a serving platter with jam. Serves 4.

1 serving: 280 Calories; 12 g Total Fat (3.5 g Mono, 0.5 g Poly, 7 g Sat); 35 mg Cholesterol; 35 g Carbohydrate (2 g Fibre, 12 g Sugar); 12 g Protein; 460 mg Sodium

HOW TO ROAST GARLIC

To roast garlic, trim 1/4 inch (6 mm) from each bulb to expose tops of cloves, leaving bulbs intact. Wrap bulbs individually in greased foil and bake in 375°F (190°C) for about 45 minutes until tender. Let stand until cool enough to handle.

Creole Crab Fondue

Put a little fire in your fondue. If you have some brave guests, hand them a bottle of hot sauce to add even more intensity to this already spicy dip. Serve with veggie sticks.

Cream cheese, softened	1/3 cup	75 mL
Mayonnaise	1/3 cup	75 mL
Finely chopped celery	3 tbsp.	45 mL
Finely chopped green onion	2 tbsp.	30 mL
Dijon mustard (with whole seeds)	1 tbsp.	15 mL
Creamed horseradish	1 tsp.	5 mL
Old Bay seasoning	1 tsp.	5 mL
Cayenne pepper	1/4 tsp.	1 mL
Crabmeat, cartilage removed	1/2 lb.	225 g
Grated mozzarella cheese	1/3 cup	75 mL
Fine dry bread crumbs	1/4 cup	60 mL

Combine first 8 ingredients. Stir in crabmeat and transfer to a 2 cup (500 mL) baking dish.

Combine cheese and bread crumbs and sprinkle over top. Bake in a 400°F (200°C) oven for about 20 minutes until bubbling and golden. Serves 6.

1 serving: 180 Calories; 13 g Total Fat (5 g Mono, 3 g Poly, 3.5 g Sat); 15 mg Cholesterol; 5 g Carbohydrate (0 g Fibre, 1 g Sugar); 8 g Protein; 430 mg Sodium

Panini Sticks with Dipping Trio

Sometimes picking up a convenience product and adding a few simple embellishments is all it takes to truly make it your own. This shareable treat is just as easy to make as it is to enjoy.

Extra-virgin olive oil	1 tbsp.	15 mL
Finely chopped fresh rosemary	1 tsp.	5 mL
Dried marjoram, crushed	1 tsp.	5 mL
Square panini breads (8 x 8 inches, 20 x 20 cm, each)	2	2
Coarse salt, sprinkle		
SUN-DRIED TOMATO DIP		
Tzatziki sauce	1/3 cup	75 mL
Sun-dried tomato pesto	2 tsp.	10 mL
Chili paste (sambal oelek)	1/4 tsp.	1 mL
LEMON AIOLI DIP		
Roasted garlic mayonnaise	1/3 cup	75 mL
Lemon juice	2 tsp.	10 mL
Grated lemon zest	1 tsp.	5 mL
TZIKI HERB DIP		
Tzatziki sauce	1/3 cup	75 mL
Chopped fresh dill	1 1/2 tsp.	7 mL
Chopped fresh mint	1 1/2 tsp.	7 mL
Lemon pepper	1/2 tsp.	2 mL

Combine first 3 ingredients and brush on panini breads. Cut into 1 inch (2.5 cm) wide strips and arrange, close together, on a baking sheet. Sprinkle with salt. Bake in a 400°F (200°C) oven for about 8 minutes until edges are crisp.

Sun-Dried Tomato Dip: Combine all 3 ingredients.

Lemon Ailoli Dip: Combine all 3 ingredients.

Tziki Herb Dip: Combine all 4 ingredients.

Serve dips with panini sticks. Serves 8.

1 serving: 230 Calories; 15 g Total Fat (1.5 g Mono, 6 g Poly, 4.5 g Sat); 25 mg Cholesterol; 18 g Carbohydrate (trace Fibre, trace Sugar); 3 g Protein; 350 mg Sodium

Sweet Polenta Fries with Chipotle Lime Dip

Dip these unique cornmeal fries in the sweet and spicy seasoning before dunking them in the perfectly complementary dip.

Sour cream	1/4 cup	60 mL
Mayonnaise	1/4 cup	60 mL
Lime juice	2 tbsp.	30 mL
Chopped fresh cilantro	2 tbsp.	30 mL
Finely chopped chipotle pepper in adobo sauce (see Tip, below)	1 1/2 tsp.	7 mL
Grated lime zest	1/2 tsp.	2 mL
Coarse (sanding) sugar	1/4 cup	60 mL
Coarse sea salt	2 tbsp.	30 mL
Ground cumin	1 tbsp.	15 mL
Ground coriander	1 1/2 tsp.	7 mL
Cayenne pepper	1/2 tsp.	2 mL
1.1 lb. (500 g) polenta roll	1	1
All-purpose flour	1/4 cup	60 mL
Cooking oil	3 cups	750 mL

Combine first 6 ingredients. Set aside.

Combine next 5 ingredients. Set aside.

Cut polenta roll into fries, about 1/2 inch (12 mm) thick. Gently toss in flour until coated.

Heat cooking oil in a large frying pan on medium-high (see How To, page 63). Shallow-fry polenta in batches, for about 5 minutes per batch, until golden. Transfer with a slotted spoon to paper towels to drain. While fries are still hot, toss with 1 tbsp. (15 mL) sugar mixture until coated. Serve with dip and remaining sugar mixture. Serves 6.

1 serving: 240 Calories; 18 g Total Fat (7 g Mono, 3.5 g Poly, 2.5 g Sat); 10 mg Cholesterol; 27 g Carbohydrate (2 g Fibre, 10 g Sugar); 3 g Protein; 2490 mg Sodium

Tip: Store any leftover chipotle peppers in an airtight container in the fridge.

Fiery Plaintain Chips with Cocomango Dip

There are few finer delights than introducing your friends to a new taste experience—such as chili-infused plantains tempered with a cool and soothing coconut and mango dip.

Large semi-ripe plantains, peeled	2	2
Cooking oil	2 tbsp.	30 mL
Chili oil	1 tbsp.	15 mL
Chili powder	1 tsp.	5 mL
Cayenne pepper	1/2 tsp.	2 mL
Finely chopped ripe mango	1/4 cup	60 mL
Sour cream	1/4 cup	60 mL
Coconut rum	2 tbsp.	30 mL
Medium unsweetened coconut, toasted (see How To, below)	2 tbsp.	30 mL
Granulated sugar	1 1/2 tsp.	7 mL
Lime juice	1 1/2 tsp.	7 mL
Ground allspice	1/8 tsp.	0.5 mL
Ground nutmeg, pinch		

Cut plantain at a sharp angle into 1/8 inch (3 mm) thick slices. Combine next 4 ingredients. Add plantain and toss gently until coated. Arrange in a single layer on 2 baking sheets lined with parchment paper. Bake in a 350°F (175°C) oven for 35 to 40 minutes, turning at halftime, until browned around edges. Let stand for 10 minutes.

Combine remaining 8 ingredients. Serve with chips. Serves 6.

1 serving: 180 Calories; 10 g Total Fat (4.5 g Mono, 2.5 g Poly, 2.5 g Sat); trace Cholesterol; 23 g Carbohydrate (2 g Fibre, 12 g Sugar); 1 g Protein; 15 mg Sodium

HOW TO TOAST NUTS

Although raw nuts are perfectly fine for noshing, toasting them brings out an aroma and depth of flavour not apparent in the raw product. To toast nuts, seeds or coconut, place them in an ungreased frying pan. Heat on medium for 3 to 5 minutes, stirring often, until golden. To bake, spread them evenly in an ungreased shallow pan. Bake in a 350°F (175°C) oven for 5 to 10 minutes, stirring or shaking often, until golden.

Curried Cheese and Fruit Wheel

Dried fruit and mango chutney make this almond-sprinkled cheese wheel a vibrant and flavoursome accompaniment for crackers, or try it with Walnut Ginger Crisps (page 38).

4 oz. (125 g) block of cream cheese, softened	1	1
Chopped dried apricot	1/4 cup	60 mL
Raisins, chopped	1/4 cup	60 mL
Madras curry paste	1 1/2 tsp.	7 mL
Finely chopped green onion	1 tsp.	5 mL
Chopped mango chutney	2 tbsp.	30 mL
Sliced natural almonds, toasted (see How To, page 14)	1 tbsp.	15 mL

Combine first 5 ingredients. Press firmly into a straight-sided 1 cup (250 mL) ramekin or bowl lined with plastic wrap. Invert onto a serving plate.

Spread with mango chutney and sprinkle with almonds. Serve immediately. Makes about 1 cup (250 mL). Serves 8.

1 serving: 90 Calories; 5 g Total Fat (0 g Mono, 0 g Poly, 3 g Sat); 15 mg Cholesterol; 10 g Carbohydrate (trace Fibre, 9 g Sugar); 1 g Protein; 140 mg Sodium

Strawberry Salsa with Goat Cheese and Melba Toast

Balsamic vinegar and pepper highlight an often-overlooked aspect of fresh strawberries—their ability to blend well with, rather than overshadow, other ingredients. Further enhanced by chèvre, this ensemble is both captivating and surprising.

Finely chopped fresh strawberries	2 cups	500 mL
White balsamic vinegar	2 tbsp.	30 mL
Minced fresh basil	1 1/2 tbsp.	25 mL
Minced fresh chives	1 1/2 tsp.	7 mL
Granulated sugar	1 tsp.	5 mL
Coarsely ground pepper	1/2 tsp.	2 mL
Soft goat (chèvre) cheese	1/4 cup	60 mL
Round Melba toasts	24	24

Combine first 6 ingredients. Let stand for 30 minutes to blend flavours.

Serve cheese with Melba toast and strawberry mixture. Serves 8.

1 serving: 70 Calories; 1.5 g Total Fat (0 g Mono, 0 g Poly, 0.5 g Sat); trace Cholesterol; 11 g Carbohydrate (2 g Fibre, 3 g Sugar); 2 g Protein; 90 mg Sodium

Roasted Spinach Portobellos

Stuffed mushrooms are always a crowd-pleaser. Using large portobellos in place of smaller mushrooms makes for a unique presentation and easier prep. Pairs perfectly with other Italian-flavoured appetizers.

Large portobello mushrooms, gills and stem removed (see Tip, below)	2	2
Butter-flavoured cooking spray		
Bacon slices, diced	2	2
Chopped fresh spinach leaves, lightly packed	2 cups	500 mL
Basil pesto	3 tbsp.	45 mL
Fine dry bread crumbs	2 tbsp.	30 mL
Grated Italian cheese blend	3/4 cup	175 mL
Pine nuts	2 tsp.	10 mL
Prepared marinara pasta sauce	1/4 cup	60 mL

Remove and chop mushroom stems. Set aside. Spray both sides of mushroom caps with cooking spray and place, stem side down, on a baking sheet. Bake in a 375°F (190°C) oven for 10 minutes.

Cook bacon in a frying pan until crisp. Add mushroom stems and cook for about 5 minutes until softened and liquid is evaporated.

Stir in spinach leaves and pesto and cook until spinach is softened. Remove from heat.

Stir in bread crumbs and half the cheese. Spoon into mushroom caps. Sprinkle with remaining cheese and pine nuts. Bake for 10 to 15 minutes until heated through and golden. Cut into quarters.

Swirl some marinara sauce on a serving plate. Arrange mushroom wedges over sauce, drizzling remaining sauce over top. Makes 8 wedges.

1 wedge: 130 Calories; 10 g Total Fat (2 g Mono, 1 g Poly, 3.5 g Sat); 15 mg Cholesterol; 5 g Carbohydrate (trace Fibre, 2 g Sugar); 6 g Protein; 280 mg Sodium

Tip: Because the gills can sometimes be bitter, remove them from the portobellos before stuffing. First remove the stems, then, using a small spoon, scrape out and discard the mushroom gills.

Wild Rice Blini

Soft little pancakes filled with chewy wild rice and tangy capers are easily made using pancake mix. Cutting small rounds from two larger pancakes is a smart shortcut for perfectly sized blini. Garnish with smoked salmon slivers and sprigs of fresh dill.

Large egg, fork-beaten	1	1
Milk	2 tbsp.	30 mL
Chopped cooked wild rice	1/4 cup	60 mL
Chopped capers	1 tbsp.	15 mL
Pepper	1/4 tsp.	1 mL
Buttermilk pancake mix	1/3 cup	75 mL
Cooking oil	2 tsp.	10 mL
Spreadable cream cheese	3 tbsp.	45 mL
Finely chopped fresh dill	1 tsp.	5 mL

Combine first 5 ingredients in a bowl. Stir in pancake mix until just mixed.

Heat cooking oil in a small frying pan on medium. Spoon half of batter into the pan, tilting and swirling pan to ensure bottom is covered. Cook for 1 to 2 minutes until edges appear dry and bubbles form on top. Turn pancake. Cook for 1 to 2 minutes until golden. Transfer to cutting board. Repeat with remaining batter. Using a 2 inch (5 cm) cookie cutter, cut out 7 circles from each pancake.

Combine cream cheese and dill. Spoon about 3/4 tsp. (4 mL) onto each circle. Makes 14 blini.

1 blini: 30 Calories; 1.5 g Total Fat (0 g Mono, 0 g Poly, 0.5 g Sat); 20 mg Cholesterol; 3 g Carbohydrate (0 g Fibre, trace Sugar); 1 g Protein; 75 mg Sodium

Tostada Cups with Lemony Lentils and Spinach

What makes this dish so conversational is the interesting use of tortilla shells to create toasty little cups. Be as inventive as you like and create your own fillings.

Flour tortilla (9 inch, 23 cm, diameter)	1	1
Cooking spray		
Cooking oil	1/2 tsp.	2 mL
Finely chopped onion	1/4 cup	60 mL
Granulated sugar	1/4 tsp.	1 mL
Canned lentils, rinsed and drained	1/2 cup	125 mL
Chopped fresh spinach leaves, lightly packed	1/2 cup	125 mL
Finely chopped roasted red pepper	2 tsp.	10 mL
Herb and garlic cream cheese	1 tbsp.	15 mL
Grated lemon zest	1 tsp.	5 mL
Salt	1/4 tsp.	1 mL
Pepper, sprinkle		

Spray both sides of tortilla with cooking spray and cut into 8 wedges. Press wedges into 8 muffin cups with points sticking out (see How To, below). Bake in a 450°F (230°C) oven for about 5 minutes until golden and crisp.

Heat cooking oil in a frying pan on medium. Add onion and sugar and cook until lightly browned.

Stir in next 3 ingredients and cook until spinach starts to wilt.

Stir in remaining 4 ingredients. Spoon into tostada cups. Makes 8 tostada cups.

1 tostada cup: 45 Calories; 1 g Total Fat (0 g Mono, 0 g Poly, 0 g Sat); 0 mg Cholesterol; 7 g Carbohydrate (trace Fibre, trace Sugar); 2 g Protein; 140 mg Sodium

HOW TO MAKE TOSTADA CUPS

Press tortilla wedges into muffin cups with points sticking out.

Potato Crostini with Caramelized Bacon

Roasted baby potatoes make for an interesting twist on traditional bread crostini. Caramelizing the bacon adds sweetness to the smokiness. Try using a combination of red and white potatoes for an appealing colour contrast.

Baby potatoes, ends trimmed and cut in half crosswise	8	8
Olive oil	1 tbsp.	15 mL
Salt	1/4 tsp.	1 mL
Brown sugar, packed	1/2 cup	125 mL
Dried crushed chilies	1 tsp.	5 mL
Bacon slices	10	10
Sour cream	1/4 cup	60 mL
Cream cheese, softened	2 tbsp.	30 mL
Dijon mustard	1/2 tsp.	2 mL
Dried crushed chilies	1/4 tsp.	1 mL

Toss first 3 ingredients together in a bowl, then spread evenly on a baking sheet. Bake in a 400°F (200°C) oven for about 25 minutes until potatoes are tender. Arrange potatoes, trimmed side down, on a serving plate. Reduce oven temperature to 350°F (175°C).

Combine brown sugar and first amount of chilies. Coat bacon slices with the brown sugar mixture. Arrange on a wire rack set in a foil-lined baking sheet. Bake for about 25 minutes until browned and glazed. Let stand for 10 minutes before finely chopping bacon.

Combine remaining 4 ingredients and bacon. Spoon onto potatoes. Makes 16 crostini.

1 crostini: 160 Calories; 13 g Total Fat (6 g Mono, 1.5 g Poly, 4.5 g Sat); 20 mg Cholesterol; 9 g Carbohydrate (0 g Fibre, 7 g Sugar); 3 g Protein; 250 mg Sodium

Pear Puff Tart

A perfect combination of sweet and savoury flavours on a bed of golden, buttery pastry. For a different presentation, serve the tart whole and allow your guests to cut their own portions.

14 oz. (397 g) package of puff pastry, thawed according to package directions	1/2	1/2
Granulated sugar	1 tbsp.	15 mL
Crumbled Stilton cheese	1/2 cup	125 mL
Medium fresh unpeeled pear, thinly sliced	1	1
Butter, melted	1 tsp.	5 mL
Coarsely ground pepper, sprinkle		

Roll out pastry to a 7 x 11 inch (18 cm x 28 cm) rectangle and transfer to a baking sheet. Sprinkle with sugar.

Sprinkle with cheese, leaving a 1/2 inch (12 mm) border. Arrange pear slices over cheese. Brush with butter and sprinkle with pepper. Bake in a 400°F (200°C) oven for 20 to 25 minutes until golden. Cut into 8 pieces.

1 piece: 190 Calories; 12 g Total Fat (6 g Mono, 1.5 g Poly, 4.5 g Sat); 10 mg Cholesterol; 16 g Carbohydrate (trace Fibre, 4 g Sugar); 4 g Protein; 180 mg Sodium

Grecian Beef Pastries

Opa! Make it a completely Greek experience by serving a rich red wine or a shot of ouzo with these sensational little pastries.

Olive oil	1 tsp.	5 mL
Lean ground beef	1/2 lb.	225 g
Chopped red onion	1/2 cup	125 mL
Chopped red pepper	1/2 cup	125 mL
Sun-dried tomato pesto	2 tbsp.	30 mL
Lemon juice	2 tsp.	10 mL
Garlic clove, minced	1	1
Salt	1/4 tsp.	1 mL
Pepper	1/2 tsp.	2 mL
Grated lemon zest	1 tsp.	5 mL
14 oz. (397 g) package of puff pastry, thawed according to package directions	1/2	1/2
Chopped pitted kalamata olives	1/4 cup	60 mL
Crumbled feta cheese	1/2 cup	125 mL
Chopped fresh oregano	1 tbsp.	15 mL

Heat olive oil in a frying pan on medium. Add next 8 ingredients and scramble-fry until beef is no longer pink. Remove from heat.

Stir in lemon zest and let stand until cool.

Roll out pastry to a 12 x 12 inch (30 x 30 cm) square. Cut into 12 rectangles and transfer to a greased baking sheet. Sprinkle with beef mixture, leaving a 1/4 inch (6 mm) border. Press down gently.

Sprinkle with olives and cheese. Bake in a 400°F (200°C) oven for about 20 minutes until pastry and cheese are golden.

Sprinkle with oregano. Makes 12 pastries.

1 pastry: 180 Calories; 13 g Total Fat (5 g Mono, 1 g Poly, 3.5 g Sat); 15 mg Cholesterol; 10 g Carbohydrate (trace Fibre, 1 g Sugar); 6 g Protein; 240 mg Sodium

Open-faced Tilapia Po'Boys

A scaled-down version of the po' boy sandwich for a taste of Mardi Gras. Serve with hot sauce on the side and cold beer or lemonade.

Large egg	1	1
Water	1 tbsp.	15 mL
Fine dry bread crumbs	1/4 cup	60 mL
Blackened (or Cajun) seasoning	1 tbsp.	15 mL
3 oz. (85 g) tilapia fillets, any small bones removed, (see Tip, below)	4	4
Cooking oil	2 tbsp.	30 mL
Mayonnaise	1/2 cup	125 mL
Tangy dill relish	2 tbsp.	30 mL
Spicy mustard (with whole seeds)	2 tbsp.	30 mL
Lemon juice	1 tbsp.	15 mL
Small dinner rolls, halved and toasted	6	6
Arugula leaves, lightly packed	1 cup	250 mL
Capers	1 tbsp.	15 mL

Beat egg and water in a shallow bowl. Combine bread crumbs and seasoning on a plate. Dip fillets into egg mixture and press into crumb mixture until coated.

Heat cooking oil in a large frying pan on medium-high. Cook fillets for about 2 minutes per side until browned and fish flakes easily when tested with a fork. Cut fillets into 3 pieces each.

Combine next 4 ingredients. Spread half of mayonnaise mixture on roll halves.

Arrange arugula and tilapia portions on roll halves. Drizzle with remaining mayonnaise mixture. Sprinkle with capers. Makes 12 po' boys.

1 po' boy: 180 Calories; 11 g Total Fat (6 g Mono, 3 g Poly, 1.5 g Sat); 35 mg Cholesterol; 10 g Carbohydrate (trace Fibre, 1 g Sugar); 8 g Protein; 510 mg Sodium

Tip: Look for the thin fillets of tilapia that are often available in the frozen section of your grocery store. If you are unable to find small fillets, you can purchase larger fillets that add up to the same weight and cut them into appropriate-sized portions after cooking.

Peanut Noodle Cakes with Sweet Chili Prawns

These curiosity-piquing noodle cakes are as much fun to make as they are to eat.

Uncooked large shrimp (peeled and deveined), butterflied (see How To, below), tails intact	12	12
Sweet chili sauce	1/3 cup	75 mL
Water	3 tbsp.	45 mL
Soy sauce	1 tbsp.	15 mL
Large egg	1	1
Chunky peanut butter	1 tbsp.	15 mL
Thai red curry paste	1 1/2 tsp.	7 mL
Cooked spaghettini	2 cups	500 mL
Chopped fresh cilantro	2 tbsp.	30 mL
Chopped green onion	2 tbsp.	30 mL
Cooking oil	3 tbsp.	45 mL

Toss first 4 ingredients together in a bowl. Let stand for 10 minutes.

Whisk next 3 ingredients together in a medium bowl. Add next 3 ingredients. Toss together until well coated.

Heat cooking oil in a large frying pan on medium. Make 6 rounds of noodle mixture in the pan. Cook for about 5 minutes per side, pressing lightly to flatten, until crispy and golden. Transfer to a plate. Add shrimp mixture to the same frying pan and cook on medium-high for about 2 minutes until shrimp turn pink. Place 2 shrimp over each noodle cake and drizzle with pan juices. Serves 6.

1 serving: 200 Calories; 9 g Total Fat (5 g Mono, 2.5 g Poly, 1 g Sat); 55 mg Cholesterol; 22 g Carbohydrate (trace Fibre, 6 g Sugar); 7 g Protein; 340 mg Sodium

HOW TO BUTTERFLY SHRIMP

To butterfly shrimp, insert a knife about three-quarters of the way into the shrimp near the head. Cut down the back to the tail so the body is divided into two attached halves.

"Uptown" Goat Cheese Potato Skins

The lowly potato skin gets an uptown makeover with the addition of lemon, capers, havarti and chèvre.

Medium unpeeled baking potatoes, baked and cooled	3	3
Olive oil	2 tbsp.	30 mL
Lemon pepper	1/2 tsp.	2 mL
Crumbled goat (chèvre) cheese	3/4 cup	175 mL
Grated havarti cheese	1/2 cup	125 mL
Butter	1 tbsp.	15 mL
Coarsely chopped capers	3 tbsp.	45 mL
Garlic cloves, thinly sliced	2	2
Sun-dried tomatoes in oil, blotted dry and finely chopped	1/3 cup	75 mL
Chopped fresh chives	2 tbsp.	30 mL
Chopped fresh oregano	1 tbsp.	15 mL

Cut potatoes into quarters lengthwise. Scoop away pulp, leaving a thin layer on each skin. Brush both sides of skins with olive oil and sprinkle with lemon pepper. Place, skin side up, on a baking sheet. Bake in a 425°F (220°C) oven for about 7 minutes until starting to crisp. Turn over.

Sprinkle goat and havarti cheese over top. Bake for about 7 minutes until cheese is melted and golden. Arrange on a serving platter.

Melt butter in a frying pan on medium. Add capers and garlic and cook for about 5 minutes until garlic is golden. Spoon over potatoes.

Sprinkle with remaining 3 ingredients. Makes 12 potato skins.

1 potato skin: 140 Calories; 9 g Total Fat (3.5 g Mono, 0 g Poly, 4.5 g Sat); 20 mg Cholesterol; 11 g Carbohydrate (1 g Fibre, trace Sugar); 5 g Protein; 200 mg Sodium

Walnut Ginger Crisps

Serve these refined crisps, enhanced with the tantalizing flavours of cardamom and ginger, with a cheese tray, custard, mousse or ice cream.

All-purpose flour	1 cup	250 mL
Minced crystallized ginger	1/3 cup	75 mL
Ground cardamom	1/2 tsp.	2 mL
Egg whites (large), room temperature (see Tip, below)	3	3
Brown sugar, packed	1/3 cup	75 mL
Walnut halves	1 1/4 cups	300 mL

Combine first 3 ingredients.

Beat egg whites and brown sugar until stiff peaks form (see How To, below). Fold in flour mixture until no dry flour remains.

Fold in walnuts and spread evenly in a greased 9 x 5 x 3 inch (23 x 12.5 x 7.5 cm) loaf pan, lined with parchment paper. Bake in a 350°F (175°C) oven for about 25 minutes until golden and firm. Transfer pan to a wire rack and let stand for 45 minutes. Remove loaf from pan. Using a serrated knife, cut into 1/8 inch (3 mm) thick slices and arrange on a baking sheet. Bake in a 300°F (150°C) oven for about 15 minutes, turning at halftime, until dry and crisp. Transfer baking sheet to a wire rack and let stand until cool. Makes about 36 crisps.

1 crisp: 60 Calories; 2.5 g Total Fat (0 g Mono, 2 g Poly, 0 g Sat); 0 mg Cholesterol; 7 g Carbohydrate (0 g Fibre, 2 g Sugar); 1 g Protein; 5 mg Sodium

Tip: It is easiest to separate your eggs when they are cold, but always beat them at room temperature.

HOW TO SPOT SOFT AND STIFF PEAKS

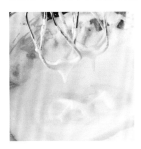 

Soft peaks are just starting to hold and will melt back into the mixture after a few seconds.

Stiff peaks hold their shape, and the mixture in the bowl will be thick.

Arugula Pesto Ravioli with Browned Butter Pine Nuts

With its inspired combination of flavours, this deconstructed, highly captivating version of ravioli eliminates the hard labour but yields delicious results.

Fresh lasagna sheets (6 x 8 inches, 15 x 20 cm, each)	3	3
Arugula leaves, lightly packed	1 cup	250 mL
Pecan halves, toasted (see How To, page 14)	1/2 cup	125 mL
Basil pesto	1/3 cup	75 mL
Grated Asiago cheese	1/4 cup	60 mL
Butter	1/4 cup	60 mL
Pine nuts	3 tbsp.	45 mL
Chopped fresh parsley	2 tsp.	10 mL
Grated lemon zest	1 tsp.	5 mL

Cook lasagna sheets in boiling salted water for about 5 minutes until softened. Drain. Rinse with cold water, draining well.

In a blender or food processor, process next 3 ingredients until smooth. Stir in cheese. Spread 1/4 of arugula mixture over 1 lasagna sheet in a greased pan. Repeat layers, spreading remaining arugula mixture over top. Cut into 8 rectangles.

Melt butter in a frying pan on medium. Add pine nuts and cook until butter is browned. Drizzle over pasta rectangles. Bake, covered, in a 400°F (200°C) oven for about 15 minutes until heated through. Transfer to a serving plate.

Sprinkle with parsley and lemon zest. Makes 8 ravioli.

1 ravioli: 220 Calories; 19 g Total Fat (5 g Mono, 3 g Poly, 6 g Sat); 20 mg Cholesterol; 11 g Carbohydrate (2 g Fibre, 2 g Sugar); 5 g Protein; 180 mg Sodium

Tapenade Toasts

A diagonal cut of a baguette can present a perfect canvas for simple, expertly chosen ingredients. This rustic arrangement belies the sophistication of flavours.

Baguette bread slices, cut at a sharp angle, about 1/2 inch (12 mm) thick	4	4
Olive oil	1 tbsp.	15 mL
Soft goat (chèvre) cheese	1/4 cup	60 mL
Black olive tapenade	1/4 cup	60 mL
Chopped fresh basil	1 tbsp.	15 mL

Arrange bread slices on a baking sheet. Brush with olive oil. Bake in a 350°F (175°C) oven for about 10 minutes until golden. Turn over and brush with olive oil. Bake for about 5 minutes until golden.

Spread with goat cheese and tapenade. Sprinkle with basil. Cut in half diagonally. Makes 8 toasts.

1 toast: 60 Calories; 3.5 g Total Fat (2 g Mono, 2 g Poly, 1 g Sat); trace Cholesterol; 5 g Carbohydrate (0 g Fibre, 0 g Sugar); 2 g Protein; 110 mg Sodium

Salty-sweet Croustades

A trip to an Italian market is bound to motivate anyone who loves to cook. This recipe was inspired by the Italian custom of combining sharp Parmigiano with the honest sweetness of honey.

Walnut halves, toasted (see How To, page 14)	12	12
Liquid honey	3 tbsp.	45 mL
Baby green leaves	12	12
Pieces of Reggiano Parmigiano cheese, about 1/4 inch (6 mm) thick, 2 inches (5 cm) long (about 1/2 oz., 43 g)	12	12
Siljan mini croustade shells (see Tip, below)	12	12
Balsamic vinegar	1 tbsp.	15 mL

Coat walnuts with honey.

Place 1 lettuce leaf, 1 piece of cheese and 1 walnut in each croustade shell.

Drizzle with balsamic vinegar. Makes 12 croustades.

1 croustade: 45 Calories; 2.5 g Total Fat (0 g Mono, 1 g Poly, 0 g Sat); trace Cholesterol; 6 g Carbohydrate (0 g Fibre, 4 g Sugar); 1 g Protein; 50 mg Sodium

Tip: Siljan croustade shells are generally found in the deli, import or cracker sections of your local grocery store.

Margarita Chicken Lollipops

With their exceptional flavour and unique presentation, these drumettes are sure to be a hit at your next get-together.

Tequila	1/2 cup	125 mL
Lime juice	1/4 cup	60 mL
Dried crushed chilies	1 tsp.	5 mL
Ground cumin	1 tsp.	5 mL
Chili powder	1/2 tsp.	2 mL
Garlic powder	1/2 tsp.	2 mL
Salt	1/2 tsp.	2 mL
Chicken drumettes, Frenched (optional), see How To, below	2 lb.	900 g
Cornstarch	2 tsp.	10 mL
Tequila	2 tbsp.	30 mL
Orange juice	1 tbsp.	15 mL
Liquid honey	1 tbsp.	15 mL
Grated lime zest	1 tsp.	5 mL

Combine first 7 ingredients in a large resealable freezer bag. Add drumettes and marinate for 4 hours. Drain marinade into a saucepan. Simmer on medium for 5 minutes.

Stir cornstarch into tequila and orange juice. Add to simmering marinade mixture and stir until bubbling and thickened. Stir in honey and lime zest. Arrange drumettes on a foil-lined baking sheet. Brush marinade mixture over drumettes. Bake in a 425°F (220°C) oven for about 20 minutes, brushing occasionally with marinade mixture, until no longer pink inside. Makes about 16 drumettes.

1 drumette: 150 Calories; 9 g Total Fat (3.5 g Mono, 2 g Poly, 2.5 g Sat); 45 mg Cholesterol; 2 g Carbohydrate (0 g Fibre, 1 g Sugar); 11 g Protein; 115 mg Sodium

HOW TO FRENCH DRUMETTES

Use a sharp knife to loosen the meat and skin from the skinny end of the drumette. Gently push the skin and meat toward the fat end, cleanly exposing the bone. Remove any bits of fat.

Crab Sushi Squares

A familiar California roll flavour with a unique and stylish presentation. Serve with pickled ginger or wasabi for the sushi enthusiasts in your crowd.

Japanese-style (sushi) rice	3/4 cup	175 mL
Water	1 cup	250 mL
Mirin	1 1/2 tbsp.	25 mL
Rice vinegar	1 1/2 tbsp.	25 mL
Granulated sugar	1 tbsp.	15 mL
Black sesame seeds	1/2 tsp.	2 mL
Salt	1/2 tsp.	2 mL
Nori (roasted seaweed) sheet	1	1
Large ripe avocado, thinly sliced	1	1
11 oz. (320 g) can of frozen crabmeat, thawed and squeezed dry, cartilage removed	1	1
Mayonnaise	3 tbsp.	45 mL
Chili paste (sambal oelek)	1 tsp.	5 mL
Black sesame seeds, sprinkle		

Combine rice and water in a small saucepan. Bring to a boil. Simmer, covered, on medium-low for 20 minutes, without stirring. Remove from heat and let stand, covered, for 10 minutes. Transfer to a bowl.

Stir next 5 ingredients until sugar is dissolved. Add to rice and mix well.

Line the bottom of an 8 x 8 inch (20 x 20 cm) baking dish with foil, allowing foil to overhang on opposite sides. Place nori sheet in baking dish, cutting to fit if necessary. Firmly press rice mixture over nori. Arrange avocado slices over top.

Combine next 3 ingredients and spread over avocado. Sprinkle with sesame seeds. Chill, covered, for 1 hour. Remove sushi from the baking dish (see How To, below) and cut into 16 squares.

1 square: 90 Calories; 3 g Total Fat (1.5 g Mono, 1 g Poly, 0 g Sat); 10 mg Cholesterol; 10 g Carbohydrate (1 g Fibre, 2 g Sugar); 4 g Protein; 260 mg Sodium

HOW TO REMOVE SUSHI

Using overhanging foil as handles, gently lift the sushi from the dish.

Spiced Panko Chicken with Tropical Rum Dip

These refined chicken fingers are paired with a coconut rum dip to ease your guests into contemplating the finer things life has to offer.

Olive oil	1/4 cup	60 mL
Dijon mustard	3 tbsp.	45 mL
Montreal steak spice	1 tsp.	5 mL
Boneless, skinless chicken breasts, cut into ten 1 inch (2.5 cm) wide strips, about 3 inches (7.5 cm) long	3/4 lb.	340 g
Panko crumbs	1 1/2 cups	375 mL
Paprika	1/2 tsp.	2 mL
Cooking spray		
Pineapple orange juice	1 1/2 cups	375 mL
Brown sugar, packed	1/4 cup	60 mL
Coconut rum	2 tbsp.	30 mL
Dijon mustard	2 tsp.	10 mL

Combine first 3 ingredients in a large resealable freezer bag. Add chicken and marinate in refrigerator for 4 hours. Drain, discarding marinade.

Combine panko crumbs and paprika. Press chicken into panko mixture until coated. Arrange on a greased wire rack set on a baking sheet. Spray with cooking spray. Bake in a 450°F (230°C) oven for about 15 minutes until crisp and no longer pink inside.

Combine juice and brown sugar in a saucepan. Boil gently on medium for about 25 minutes until thickened to a syrup consistency. Remove from heat.

Stir in rum and mustard. Serve with chicken. Serves 10.

1 serving: 140 Calories; 3 g Total Fat (2 g Mono, 0 g Poly, 0 g Sat); 20 mg Cholesterol; 16 g Carbohydrate (trace Fibre, 7 g Sugar); 9 g Protein; 120 mg Sodium

Walnut Pesto-crusted Lamb with Cranberry Port Jus

Treat your guests with these delicate walnut-crusted chops nestled in a fruity jus. Simple to prepare yet sophisticated and oh so delicious!

Rack of lamb (8 ribs), bones Frenched (see Tip, below)	1	1
Salt, sprinkle		
Pepper, sprinkle		
Cooking oil	1 tsp.	5 mL
Ruby port	1 cup	250 mL
Cranberries	1/2 cup	125 mL
Balsamic vinegar	2 tsp.	10 mL
Whole wheat bread slice	1	1
Chopped walnuts, toasted (see How To, page 14)	2 tbsp.	30 mL
Basil pesto	1 tsp.	5 mL
Butter, melted	1 tbsp.	15 mL
Dijon mustard	1 tbsp.	15 mL

Cover exposed bones of lamb rack with foil (so they won't darken during roasting). Sprinkle lamb with salt and pepper. Heat cooking oil in a frying pan on medium-high. Sear lamb until browned. Transfer to a greased baking sheet.

Add port and cranberries to the pan. Boil gently until reduced by half. Stir in vinegar. Transfer to a blender or food processor and process until smooth.

In a clean blender or food processor, process bread into coarse crumbs. Add walnuts and pesto and process until just combined. Transfer to a bowl. Drizzle with butter and toss until combined.

Brush meaty side of lamb with mustard. Press crumb mixture over the mustard. Bake, uncovered, in a 375°F (190°C) oven for 20 to 25 minutes until internal temperature reaches 135°F (57°C) or until meat reaches desired doneness. Cover with foil and let stand for 10 minutes. Cut lamb rack into 1-bone portions and serve with cranberry mixture. Serves 8.

1 serving: 190 Calories; 11 g Total Fat (3.5 g Mono, 1.5 g Poly, 4.5 g Sat); 20 mg Cholesterol; 9 g Carbohydrate (trace Fibre, 0 g Sugar); 6 g Protein; 75 mg Sodium

Tip: When getting your lamb rack cut, ask the butcher to remove the chine bone (the backbone). The ribs will be easier to slice and separate.

Shrimp Corn Cakes with Lime Sauce

Ever-popular southwestern flavours add a contemporary and appetizing twist. These refreshing and delicious cakes are best served with margaritas, beer or tequila.

Large egg	1	1
Chopped cooked shrimp (peeled and deveined)	1 cup	250 mL
Finely chopped kernel corn	1/2 cup	125 mL
All-purpose flour	2 tbsp.	30 mL
Chopped fresh cilantro	2 tbsp.	30 mL
Yellow cornmeal	2 tbsp.	30 mL
Sour cream	1 tbsp.	15 mL
Seasoned salt	1/2 tsp.	2 mL
Butter	2 tbsp.	30 mL
Lime juice	2 tsp.	10 mL
Minced chipotle pepper in adobo sauce (see Tip, below)	1 1/2 tsp.	7 mL

Whisk egg until frothy. Stir in next 7 ingredients to form a thick batter.

Melt about 1 tbsp. (15 mL) butter in a large frying pan on medium. Drop 1 tbsp. (15 mL) portions of batter into pan. Cook for 1 to 2 minutes per side until golden. Transfer cakes to a serving platter and keep warm in a 200°F (95°C) oven. Repeat with remaining batter, adding butter between batches to prevent sticking.

Combine lime juice and chipotle pepper. Drizzle over corn cakes and serve immediately. Makes about 12 corn cakes.

1 cake: 70 Calories; 3.5 g Total Fat (1 g Mono, 0 g Poly, 1.5 g Sat); 65 mg Cholesterol; 4 g Carbohydrate (0 g Fibre, 0 g Sugar); 7 g Protein; 130 mg Sodium

Tip: Store any leftover chipotle peppers in an airtight container in the fridge.

Braised Hoisin Spareribs

Hoisin and five-spice powder lend an aromatic Asian influence to these small morsels with a lively chili heat. Serve with finger bowls so your guests can engage in a more refined eating experience.

Sweet-and-sour-cut pork ribs (breastbone removed)	1 1/2 lbs.	680 g
Hoisin sauce	1/4 cup	60 mL
Sweet chili sauce	1/4 cup	60 mL
Sesame oil	2 tbsp.	30 mL
Soy sauce	2 tbsp.	30 mL
Water	2 tbsp.	30 mL
Garlic cloves, minced	2	2
Chinese five-spice powder	1 tsp.	5 mL

Place ribs, bone side down, in a baking pan.

Stir remaining 7 ingredients until smooth. Pour 2/3 cup (150 mL) of sauce mixture over ribs. Bake, covered, in a 350°F (175°C) oven for 30 minutes. Bake, uncovered, for about 45 minutes, basting with pan juices and remaining sauce mixture, until fully cooked and tender. Cover with foil and let stand for 10 minutes. Transfer to cutting board and cut ribs into 1-bone portions. Makes about 12 ribs.

1 rib: 200 Calories; 16 g Total Fat (1 g Mono, 1 g Poly, 4.5 g Sat); 45 mg Cholesterol; 5 g Carbohydrate (0 g Fibre, 2 g Sugar); 9 g Protein; 320 mg Sodium

Smoked Tuna and Wasabi Cream in Endive Boats

Red-orange pearls of caviar provide a glorious garnish to the artful display of smoked tuna on an endive leaf. The contrasting tastes and textures meld beautifully.

Paper-thin English cucumber slices (with peel)	36	36
Rice vinegar	1 tbsp.	15 mL
Granulated sugar	1 tsp.	10 mL
Salt	1/4 tsp.	1 mL
Sour cream	2 tbsp.	30 mL
Grated lime zest	1 1/4 tsp.	6 mL
Wasabi paste	3/4 tsp.	4 mL
Medium Belgian endive leaves	12	12
4 1/2 oz. (120 g) can of smoked light tuna slices, drained	1	1

Combine first 4 ingredients. Let stand for 10 minutes.

Combine next 3 ingredients.

Arrange endive on a serving plate. Arrange 3 overlapping cucumber slices on 1 end of each leaf. Top with a half slice of tuna. Spoon wasabi mixture over top. Makes 12 endive boats.

1 boat: 25 Calories; 1 g Total Fat (0 g Mono, 0 g Poly, 0 g Sat); 0 mg Cholesterol; 5 g Carbohydrate (2 g Fibre, trace Sugar); 3 g Protein; 100 mg Sodium

Herb Olive Feta Mélange over Grilled Asparagus

A topping of herbs, olives and feta provides a complex contrast to the simple, fresh flavour of grilled asparagus.

Fresh asparagus, trimmed of tough ends	1 lb.	454 g
Olive oil	1 tbsp.	15 mL
Salt, sprinkle		
Pepper, sprinkle		
Diced feta cheese	1/3 cup	75 mL
Large pitted green olives	1/3 cup	75 mL
Large pitted kalamata olives	1/3 cup	75 mL
Chopped fresh basil	1 tbsp.	15 mL
Chopped fresh oregano	1 tbsp.	15 mL
Chopped fresh rosemary	1 tsp.	5 mL
Roasted garlic olive oil	2 tbsp.	30 mL

Toss asparagus in olive oil and sprinkle with salt and pepper. Cook on a greased grill on medium for about 5 minutes, turning occasionally, until browned. Arrange on a serving platter.

Sprinkle with next 6 ingredients. Drizzle with garlic olive oil. Serves 6.

1 serving: 130 Calories; 12 g Total Fat (6 g Mono, 1 g Poly, 2 g Sat); 5 mg Cholesterol; 5 g Carbohydrate (2 g Fibre, 2 g Sugar); 3 g Protein; 410 mg Sodium

Halibut Bites in Peppered Panko Crust

A welcome, yet unexpected offering at any gathering, these cubes of pure-white halibut are encased in a peppery, crisp golden crust. Your guests will delight in their uniqueness.

All-purpose flour	3 tbsp.	45 mL
Seasoned salt	1/2 tsp.	2 mL
Large egg	1	1
Lemon juice	1 tbsp.	15 mL
Panko bread crumbs	1 cup	250 mL
Coarsely ground pepper	1 tbsp.	15 mL
Halibut fillets (any small bones removed), cut into 1 inch (2.5 cm) pieces	3/4 lb.	340 g
Cooking oil	3 cups	750 mL
Coarse sea salt	1 tsp.	5 mL
Grated lemon zest	1 tsp.	5 mL

Combine flour and seasoned salt in a large resealable freezer bag.

Beat egg and lemon juice in a small shallow bowl.

Combine panko crumbs and pepper in a separate large resealable freezer bag.

Toss halibut cubes in flour mixture until coated. Dip into egg mixture, then toss in crumb mixture until coated.

Heat cooking oil in a large frying pan on medium (see How To, page 63). Shallow-fry halibut for about 2 minutes, turning once, until golden. Transfer with a slotted spoon to a plate lined with paper towel to drain.

Sprinkle with sea salt and lemon zest. Makes about 24 bites.

1 bite: 70 Calories; 5 g Total Fat (3 g Mono, 1.5 g Poly, 0 g Sat); 15 mg Cholesterol; 3 g Carbohydrate (0 g Fibre, 0 g Sugar); 4 g Protein; 135 mg Sodium

HOW TO TEST OIL TEMPERATURE

Keep your fried foods crisp, rather than greasy, with properly heated oil that has reached 350 – 375°F (170 – 190°C). The easiest way to test the temperature is to use a deep-fry thermometer. If you don't have a thermometer, try either of the following:

• Insert the tip of a wooden spoon. If the oil around it bubbles, the temperature is right.

• Toss in a small piece of bread. If it sizzles and turns brown within 1 minute, the oil is ready.

Ginger Chicken Dumplings

Reminiscent of dim sum fare but far more visually stimulating, these beauties are certain to spark conversation.

Lean ground chicken	6 oz.	170 g
Finely chopped green onion	1 tbsp.	15 mL
Finely grated carrot	1 tbsp.	15 mL
Minced red pepper	1 tbsp.	15 mL
Oyster sauce	2 tsp.	10 mL
Cornstarch	1 tsp.	5 mL
Finely grated ginger root	1 tsp.	5 mL
Garlic clove, minced	1	1
Soy sauce	1 tsp.	5 mL
Round dumpling wrappers	8	8
Suey choy (Chinese cabbage) leaves	2	2
Hoisin sauce	1 tbsp.	15 mL
Water	1 tbsp.	15 mL

Combine first 9 ingredients.

Spoon chicken mixture onto centres of dumpling wrappers. Dampen edges with water. Gather up edges around filling, leaving tops open. Tap dumplings gently on work surface to flatten bottoms slightly.

Line bottom of a large bamboo steamer with suey choy leaves. Arrange dumplings so they do not touch each other or the sides of the steamer. Place steamer on a rack set over simmering water in a wok or Dutch oven. Cook, covered, for about 15 minutes until filling is no longer pink and temperature reaches 175°F (80°C).

Combine hoisin sauce and water and drizzle over dumplings. Makes 8 dumplings.

1 dumpling: 60 Calories; 3 g Total Fat (0 g Mono, 0 g Poly, 0 g Sat); 20 mg Cholesterol; 4 g Carbohydrate (0 g Fibre, trace Sugar); 4 g Protein; 160 mg Sodium

Mushroom Risotto Balls

Inspired by the Italian taste sensation arancini *(food with a crisp outside and a soft, cheesy interior), these golden mushroom risotto balls have creamy Asiago tucked into the centre.*

Cooking oil	1 tsp.	5 mL
Finely chopped white mushrooms	1 cup	250 mL
Minced onion	1/2 cup	125 mL
Arborio rice	1/2 cup	125 mL
Dry white wine	1/4 cup	60 mL
Hot prepared vegetable broth	1 1/3 cups	325 mL
Pepper	1/4 tsp.	1 mL
Grated Parmesan cheese	1/4 cup	60 mL
Grated lemon zest	1/2 tsp.	2 mL
Asiago cheese cubes (1/2 inch, 12 mm, each)	12	12
All-purpose flour	2 tbsp.	30 mL
Cooking oil	3 cups	750 mL
Prepared rosé pasta sauce, warmed	1/2 cup	125 mL

Heat cooking oil in a saucepan on medium. Add mushrooms and onion and cook until softened. Add rice. Heat and stir for 30 seconds.

Add wine. Cook until wine is almost all evaporated. Stir in hot broth and pepper. Bring to a boil. Simmer, covered, on medium-low for about 15 minutes, without stirring, until rice is tender and liquid is absorbed.

Stir in Parmesan cheese and lemon zest. Spoon 2 tbsp. (30 mL) portions of risotto mixture onto a waxed paper-lined baking sheet. Let stand for 5 minutes to cool.

Place 1 Asiago cheese cube on each risotto mound. With wet hands, roll into balls, enclosing cheese. Lightly toss in flour.

Heat cooking oil in a large frying pan on medium-high (see How To, page 63). Shallow-fry risotto balls for 2 to 3 minutes, turning occasionally, until golden and heated through. Transfer to a plate lined with paper towel. Let stand for 2 minutes.

Drizzle pasta sauce on a serving plate. Arrange risotto balls over sauce. Makes about 12 risotto balls.

1 risotto ball: 140 Calories; 9 g Total Fat (3 g Mono, 1.5 g Poly, 2.5 g Sat); 10 mg Cholesterol; 10 g Carbohydrate (0 g Fibre, 2 g Sugar); 4 g Protein; 250 mg Sodium

Chicken Saltimbocca Spikes

Full Italian flavours of fresh sage and prosciutto complement Marsala's fortified sweetness. With a finishing touch of lemon the creation is complete.

Finely chopped fresh sage	2 tbsp.	30 mL
Pepper	1/8 tsp.	0.5 mL
Chicken breast fillets, cut crosswise into 3 pieces each	1/2 lb.	225 g
Prosciutto ham slices, cut lengthwise into 1 inch (2.5 cm) wide strips	3 oz.	85 g
Fresh sage leaves	8	8
Butter, melted	2 tbsp.	30 mL
Extra-virgin olive oil	1 tbsp.	15 mL
Marsala wine	2 tbsp.	30 mL
Bamboo cocktail picks or skewers	18	18
Lemon juice	2 tbsp.	30 mL

Sprinkle sage and pepper on chicken. Roll 1 prosciutto strip around each chicken piece. Place, seam side down, in a baking dish.

Scatter sage leaves over rolls. Drizzle with butter and olive oil. Bake in a 450°F (230°C) oven for 4 minutes. Drizzle with marsala. Bake for about 4 minutes until internal temperature reaches 175°F (80°C).

Skewer rolls. Drizzle with lemon juice and pan juices. Makes about 18 spikes.

1 spike: 50 Calories; 3 g Total Fat (1 g Mono, 0 g Poly, 1 g Sat); 15 mg Cholesterol; 1 g Carbohydrate (trace Fibre, 0 g Sugar); 4 g Protein; 105 mg Sodium

Leek-wrapped Ginger Scallops with Soy Glaze

Whereas bacon-wrapped scallops may be too much of a good thing, leek-wrapped scallops provide the perfect light compromise. The inclusion of ginger and a salty-sweet glaze finish off this appetizer perfectly.

Soy sauce	1/2 cup	125 mL
Brown sugar, packed	2 tbsp.	30 mL
Large leek (white part only), trimmed to 5 inches (12.5 cm)	1	1
Pickled ginger slices, halved	6	6
Large sea scallops	12	12
Wooden cocktail picks	12	12
Water	1/2 cup	125 mL
Soy sauce	2 tbsp.	30 mL

Combine first amount of soy sauce and brown sugar in a saucepan. Simmer on medium-low for about 5 minutes until reduced to a syrupy consistency.

Remove 12 leaves from centre of leek. Blanch in boiling water for 1 minute to soften. Drain and plunge into ice water for 1 minute. Drain well and blot dry.

Roll 1 ginger piece and 1 scallop in each leaf. Secure with cocktail picks (see How To, below).

Combine water and second amount of soy sauce in a frying pan. Bring to a simmer on medium and add skewers. Cook, covered, for about 4 minutes until scallops are opaque. Transfer to a serving plate using a slotted spoon. Serve with brown sugar mixture. Makes 12 skewers.

1 skewers: 25 Calories; 0 g Total Fat (0 g Mono, 0 g Poly, 0 g Sat); trace Cholesterol; 1 g Carbohydrate (0 g Fibre, 0 g Sugar); 4 g Protein; 790 mg Sodium

HOW TO ASSEMBLE SCALLOP ROLLS

Arrange leek leaves on a work surface. Place one pickled ginger slice and one scallop on one end of each leaf. Roll up leaf to enclose. Secure with a cocktail pick.

Calabrese Bites

Evocative of a sunny Italian countryside picnic, these exceptional salami and bocconcini bites combine many of the fresh flavours so characteristic of Tuscany.

Calabrese salami slices, halved (about 2 oz., 57 g)	6	6
Medium fresh basil leaves	12	12
Cherry tomatoes, halved	6	6
Small bocconcini cheese balls	12	12
Pieces of sun-dried tomato in oil, about 1/2 inch (12 mm) each	12	12
Wooden cocktail picks	12	12
Balsamic vinegar	1 tbsp.	15 mL
Coarsely ground pepper, sprinkle		

Arrange salami on work surface, placing 1 basil leaf over each piece. Place next 3 ingredients in a row over top. Fold up ends of salami and insert a wooden pick from end to end to secure (see How To, below). Place on a baking sheet.

Drizzle with balsamic vinegar. Bake in a 400°F (200°C) oven for about 3 minutes until hot. Sprinkle with pepper and serve immediately. Makes 12 bites.

1 bite: 100 Calories; 9 g Total Fat (0 g Mono, 0 g Poly, 4.5 g Sat); 25 mg Cholesterol; trace Carbohydrate (0 g Fibre, 0 g Sugar); 6 g Protein; 100 mg Sodium

HOW TO ASSEMBLE BITES

Arrange salami slices on work surface and place a basil leaf, cherry tomato half, cheese ball and tomato slice in the centre of each slice. Fold ends of salami slice over toppings and secure with a wooden pick.

Prosciutto-wrapped Bread Sticks with Cantaloupe Purée

This modernized version of classic proscuitto-wrapped melon perfectly balances the salty ham with the invigorating sweetness of the cantaloupe purée. The varied textures also add a sensual dimension to the flavour experience.

Coarsely chopped ripe cantaloupe	1 cup	250 mL
Ground cinnamon, to taste		
Thin slices of prosciutto ham	8	8
(about 4 oz., 113 g)		
Bread sticks	8	8

In a blender or food processor, process cantaloupe and cinnamon until smooth. Pour into 8 small glasses.

Wrap 1 slice of prosciutto around 1 end of each breadstick. Place 1 bread stick across rim of each glass. Serve immediately. Serves 8.

1 serving: 50 Calories; 2 g Total Fat (0 g Mono, 0 g Poly,1 g Sat); 15 mg Cholesterol; 4 g Carbohydrate (0 g Fibre, 2 g Sugar); 5 g Protein; 310 mg Sodium

Nut, Cheese and Fruit Bites

This colourful appetizer is only one example of how you can showcase your own exquisite culinary style. Serve your favourite fruits, cheeses and nuts in unlimited combinations.

Mixed baby greens	1 cup	250 mL
Small fresh strawberries, stems removed	12	12
Soft goat (chèvre) cheese	1/3 cup	75 mL
Large unpeeled pear, cut into 1/4 inch (6 mm) slices	1	1
Lemon juice	1 tbsp.	15 mL
Blue cheese, crumbled	3/4 cup	175 mL
Pecans, walnuts and hazelnuts, toasted (see How To, page 14)	1 cup	250 mL

Arrange mixed greens on a serving tray.

Make 2 crosscuts from the tip of each strawberry, almost, but not quite, through to the base. Spread cuts open and fill with goat cheese. Arrange over greens.

Toss pear slices in lemon juice. Top slices with blue cheese. Arrange over greens. Arrange nuts over fruit. Serves 6.

1 serving: 240 Calories; 20 g Total Fat (8 g Mono, 5 g Poly, 5 g Sat); 15 mg Cholesterol; 11 g Carbohydrate (3 g Fibre, 5 g Sugar); 8 g Protein; 270 mg Sodium

Hot and Smoky Stuffed Dates

Never has a more varied grouping of flavours and textures come together in such a small package. Experience salty, smoky, spicy, sweet, soft, chewy and crunchy sensations in a virtual tempest of taste.

Medjool fresh whole dates, pitted	6	6
Real bacon bits	1 1/2 tsp.	7 mL
Asian chili sauce	3/4 tsp.	4 mL
Pieces of jalapeño Monterey Jack cheese, 1/4 inch (6 mm) thick, 1 1/2 inches (3.8 cm) long (about 3/4 oz., 21 g)	6	6
Roasted, salted smoked almonds	12	12

Stuff each date with 1/4 tsp. (1 mL) bacon bits, 1/8 tsp. (0.5 mL) chili sauce and 1 piece of cheese. Place on a baking sheet.

Top with 2 almonds each. Bake in a 375°F (190°C) oven for about 10 minutes until cheese is melted. Let stand until slightly cooled. Serve with additional chili sauce. Makes 6 stuffed dates.

1 stuffed date: 90 Calories; 2 g Total Fat (0 g Mono, 0 g Poly, 0.5 g Sat); trace Cholesterol; 19 g Carbohydrate (2 g Fibre, 16 g Sugar); 2 g Protein; 50 mg Sodium

Dukkah Beef Skewers with Wine Reduction

Aromatic spices, seeds and nuts combine to make an exotic coating with as much texture as taste. Expect an exhilarating eating experience reminiscent of Middle Eastern tradition.

Balsamic vinegar	1/4 cup	60 mL
Dry red wine	1/4 cup	60 mL
Liquid honey	1/4 cup	60 mL
Hazelnuts (filberts)	14	14
Sesame seeds	2 tsp.	10 mL
Coriander seed	1 tsp.	5 mL
Cumin seed	1 tsp.	5 mL
Grated Reggiano Parmigiano cheese	2 tbsp.	30 mL
Coarsely ground pepper	1/4 tsp.	1 mL
Olive oil	2 tbsp.	30 mL
Dijon mustard	1 tbsp.	15 mL
Beef strip loin steak, cut into 1/4 inch (6 mm) slices	3/4 lb.	340 g
Bamboo skewers (8 inches, 20 cm), soaked in water for 10 minutes	16	16

Combine first 3 ingredients in a saucepan. Boil gently on medium for about 7 minutes until reduced by half.

Heat and stir next 4 ingredients in a frying pan on medium until toasted and fragrant. Let stand until cool. Transfer to a blender or food processor and process until coarsely ground.

Combine mixture with cheese and pepper on a plate.

Combine olive oil and mustard. Add beef and stir. Thread onto skewers and press into cheese mixture until coated. Cook on a greased grill on medium-high for 1 to 2 minutes per side until meat reaches desired doneness. Drizzle half of wine mixture over top. Serve immediately with remaining wine mixture. Makes 16 skewers.

1 serving: 90 Calories; 4.5 g Total Fat (3 g Mono, 0 g Poly, 1 g Sat); 10 mg Cholesterol; 6 g Carbohydrate (0 g Fibre, 5 g Sugar); 6 g Protein; 40 mg Sodium

Thai Chicken on Lemon Grass Skewers

Fragrant lemon flavour permeates curry-flavoured chicken from the inside out with the help of lemon grass skewers.

Lean ground chicken	3/4 lb.	340 g
Fine dry bread crumbs	2/3 cup	150 mL
Brown sugar, packed	1 tbsp.	15 mL
Chopped fresh cilantro	1 tbsp.	15 mL
Minced lemon grass, bulb only (root and stalk removed)	1 tbsp.	15 mL
Thai green curry paste	1 tbsp.	15 mL
Garlic clove, minced	1	1
Stalks of lemon grass, outer layers removed	6	6
Sesame oil	2 tbsp.	30 mL

Combine first 7 ingredients.

Press about 1/4 cup (60 mL) chicken mixture around each lemon grass stalk, about 1 inch (2.5 cm) from thick end. Brush with sesame oil. Cook on a greased grill on medium-high for about 15 minutes, turning often, until chicken is no longer pink (see Tip, below). Makes 6 skewers.

1 serving: 220 Calories; 14 g Total Fat (2 g Mono, 2 g Poly, 1 g Sat); 45 mg Cholesterol; 12 g Carbohydrate (1 g Fibre, 2 g Sugar); 11 g Protein; 220 mg Sodium

Tip: When grilling the skewers, make sure the lemongrass stalk ends are away from the heat. If the ends are too close to the fire or burner, they will be scorched.

Rosemary-spiked Meatballs

Rosemary's heady aroma permeates the air when its sprigs stand in place of skewers for these Greek-inspired lamb meatballs. A tzatziki dip would be the perfect accompaniment.

Lean ground lamb	1/2 lb.	225 g
Grated Greek Myzithra cheese	1/4 cup	60 mL
Large egg, fork-beaten	1	1
Sun-dried tomato pesto	2 tsp.	10 mL
Grated lemon zest	1 tsp.	5 mL
Chopped fresh rosemary	1 tsp.	5 mL
Sprigs of fresh rosemary (6 inches, 15 cm, each), see Tip, below	4	4

Combine first 6 ingredients. Roll into 12 balls and place on a baking sheet. Bake in a 400°F (200°C) oven for about 12 minutes until internal temperature reaches 160°F (70°C). Let stand until cool enough to handle.

Thread 3 meatballs onto each rosemary sprig. Makes 4 skewers.

1 serving: 240 Calories; 19 g Total Fat (6 g Mono, 1 g Poly, 8 g Sat); 105 mg Cholesterol; 1 g Carbohydrate (0 g Fibre, trace Sugar); 15 g Protein; 600 mg Sodium

Tip: When preparing your rosemary skewers, remove all the leaves, except for those on the last two inches of each stem. Use the removed leaves in the recipe.

Mahogany Chicken Waves

A cocoa and smoked sweet paprika rub lends a becoming mahogany hue to thin strips of chicken threaded in waves. The presentation is memorable, and so is the bittersweet taste.

Brown sugar, packed	2 tbsp.	30 mL
Chili powder	1 tbsp.	15 mL
Smoked sweet paprika	1 tbsp.	15 mL
Cocoa, sifted if lumpy	1 tsp.	5 mL
Garlic powder	1/4 tsp.	1 mL
Pepper	1/4 tsp.	1 mL
4 oz. (113 g) boneless, skinless chicken breast halves, cut lengthwise into 4 strips	2	2
Bamboo skewers (8 inches, 20 cm), soaked in water for 10 minutes	8	8
Olive oil	1 tbsp.	15 mL
Salt	1/2 tsp.	2 mL

Combine first 6 ingredients. Add chicken and stir. Chill, covered, for 1 hour.

Thread chicken onto skewers. Brush with olive oil and sprinkle with salt. Cook on a greased grill on medium for about 3 minutes per side until no longer pink inside. Makes 8 skewers.

1 serving: 80 Calories; 2.5 g Total Fat (1.5 g Mono, 0 g Poly, 0 g Sat); 20 mg Cholesterol; 5 g Carbohydrate (trace Fibre, 3 g Sugar); 9 g Protein; 180 mg Sodium

Beef with Pineapple Mustard

Although the simple beef skewers will be done to perfection, it is the accompanying condiment that will take centre stage. Try it with chicken and pork as well.

Pineapple juice	2 cups	500 mL
Brown sugar, packed	1/4 cup	60 mL
Dijon mustard	2 tbsp.	30 mL
Salt	1/8 tsp.	0.5 mL
Pepper	1/4 tsp.	1 mL
Cooking oil	1 tsp.	5 mL
Seasoned salt	1/2 tsp.	2 mL
Pepper	1/4 tsp.	1 mL
Beef tenderloin, trimmed and cut into 1 inch (2.5 cm) cubes	1/2 lb.	225 g
Pineapple pieces (1 inch, 2.5 cm, each)	12	12
Bamboo skewers (8 inches, 20 cm, each), soaked in water for 10 minutes	4	4

Combine pineapple juice and sugar in a saucepan. Boil gently on medium for about 30 minutes until reduced to about 1/2 cup (125 mL).

Stir in next 3 ingredients. Reserve half of mustard mixture.

Combine next 3 ingredients. Add beef and toss.

Thread beef and pineapple onto skewers. Cook on a greased grill on medium-high for about 6 minutes, turning once and brushing with remaining mustard mixture, until they reach desired doneness. Serve with reserved mustard mixture. Makes 4 skewers.

1 serving: 270 Calories; 12 g Total Fat (5 g Mono, 0.5 g Poly, 4.5 g Sat); 40 mg Cholesterol; 31 g Carbohydrate (0 g Fibre, 26 g Sugar); 11 g Protein; 400 mg Sodium

Chili-crusted Medallions

Made to be dipped, these miniature shrimp and pork patties have a fiery presence that begs for the relief of cool yogurt. Not for the faint-hearted, these small eats should be reserved for your most flame-proofed guests.

Large egg, fork-beaten	1	1
Lean ground pork	1/2 lb.	225 g
Uncooked shrimp (peeled and deveined), coarsely chopped	6 oz.	170 g
Fine dry bread crumbs	1/4 cup	60 mL
Cornstarch	1 tbsp.	15 mL
Seasoned salt	1/2 tsp.	2 mL
Chili paste (sambal oelek)	1/4 cup	60 mL
Wooden cocktail skewers	12	12
Plain yogurt	1/2 cup	125 mL

Combine first 6 ingredients. Shape into twelve 2 inch (5 cm) diameter patties and place on a greased baking sheet. Brush with chili paste. Broil for about 3 minutes until browned. Turn and brush with chili paste. Broil for about 4 minutes until browned and internal temperature reaches 160°F (70°C). Let stand for 5 minutes.

Insert cocktail skewers and place on a serving plate. Serve with yogurt. Makes 12 skewers.

1 serving: 80 Calories; 4 g Total Fat (0 g Mono, 0 g Poly, 1.5 g Sat); 50 mg Cholesterol; 3 g Carbohydrate (0 g Fibre, 2 g Sugar); 7 g Protein; 240 mg Sodium

Sesame Chili Vegetable Skewers

These chili and ginger-basted vegetable skewers provide a colourful complement to any array of small plates. The crisp pieces of jicama are especially well-suited to the Asian-inspired baste.

Red pepper pieces, 1 inch (2.5 cm) each	32	32
Peeled jicama pieces, 1 inch (2.5 cm) wide, 1/4 inch (6 mm) thick	8	8
Small whole white mushrooms	8	8
Onion pieces, 1 inch (2.5 cm) each	8	8
Zucchini slices (with peel), 1/2 inch (12 mm) thick	8	8
Bamboo skewers (6 inches, 15 cm, each), soaked in water for 10 minutes	8	8
Sesame oil	1/3 cup	75 mL
Thai hot chili pepper (see Tip, below), minced	1	1
Finely grated ginger root	2 tsp.	10 mL
Granulated sugar	2 tsp.	10 mL
Salt	1/2 tsp.	2 mL

Thread first 5 ingredients onto skewers.

Combine remaining 5 ingredients. Cook skewers on a greased grill on medium for 10 to 15 minutes, brushing occasionally with sesame oil mixture, until vegetables are tender-crisp. Brush with sesame oil mixture and transfer to a serving plate. Makes 8 skewers.

1 serving: 100 Calories; 9 g Total Fat (3.5 g Mono, 4 g Poly, 1.5 g Sat); 0 mg Cholesterol; 6 g Carbohydrate (1 g Fibre, 4 g Sugar); 1 g Protein; 150 mg Sodium

Tip: Hot peppers contain capsaicin in the seeds and ribs, so removing them will reduce the amount of heat. When handling hot peppers, avoid touching your eyes. Be sure to wash your hands well afterwards.

Tuna Skewers

Perhaps the ultimate in decadent barbecue fare, these pistachio-crusted tuna skewers are sure to be met with delighted exclamations of approval.

Soy sauce	2 tbsp.	30 mL
Sesame oil	2 tbsp.	30 mL
Pepper	1/2 tsp.	2 mL
Tuna steak, cut into 1 inch (2.5 cm) cubes	1 lb.	454 g
Finely chopped pistachios toasted (see How To, page 14)	1/2 cup	125 mL
Bamboo skewers (8 inches, 20 cm, each), soaked in water for 10 minutes	6	6

Combine first 3 ingredients in a large resealable freezer bag. Add tuna and marinate for 30 minutes in refrigerator. Drain, discarding marinade.

Press tuna into pistachios until coated. Thread onto skewers. Cook on a greased grill on medium-high for about 1 minute per side until browned. Makes 6 skewers.

1 serving: 210 Calories; 13 g Total Fat (5 g Mono, 4.5 g Poly, 2 g Sat); 30 mg Cholesterol; 3 g Carbohydrate (1 g Fibre, trace Sugar); 20 g Protein; 340 mg Sodium

Bourbon Chicken Skewers

Drenched in a cayenne, citrus and bourbon marinade, these skewers are bound to evoke images of sultry southern nights.

Orange juice	1 cup	250 mL
Brown sugar, packed	1/4 cup	60 mL
Bourbon whiskey	1/4 cup	60 mL
Soy sauce	2 tbsp.	30 mL
Cayenne pepper	1/4 tsp.	1 mL
3 oz. (85 g) boneless, skinless chicken thighs, cut in half lengthwise	4	4
Bamboo skewers (8 inches, 20 cm, each), soaked in water for 10 minutes	8	8

Combine first 5 ingredients in a medium resealable freezer bag. Add chicken and marinate in refrigerator for at least 6 hours or overnight. Drain marinade into a saucepan. Boil gently on medium for about 20 minutes until thickened and syrupy.

Thread chicken onto skewers. Cook on a greased grill on medium for about 8 minutes, turning once and brushing with marinade, until no longer pink inside. Makes 8 skewers.

1 serving: 130 Calories; 2.5 g Total Fat (0 g Mono, 0 g Poly, 2.5 g Sat); 40 mg Cholesterol; 11 g Carbohydrate (trace Fibre, 11 Sugar); 11 g Protein; 230 mg Sodium

Pork Souvlaki with Red Pepper Yogurt

Cooked traditionally on skewers, this simple Greek fare is elevated to gourmet proportions with an accompanying yogurt dip flavoured with savoury roasted red peppers and Mediterranean seasonings.

Red wine	1/4 cup	60 mL
Olive oil	3 tbsp.	45 mL
Greek seasoning	2 tbsp.	30 mL
Garlic cloves, minced	3	3
Lemon juice	1 tbsp.	15 mL
Pork tenderloin, cut into 1 inch (2.5 cm) pieces	3/4 lb.	340 g
Bamboo skewers (4 inches, 10 cm, each), soaked in water for 10 minutes	6	6
Greek pita breads (7 inch, 18 cm, diameter)	3	3
Plain yogurt	1/2 cup	125 mL
Chopped roasted red pepper	2 tbsp.	30 mL
Greek seasoning	1 tbsp.	15 mL

Combine first 5 ingredients in a medium resealable freezer bag. Add pork and marinate in refrigerator for 2 hours. Drain, discarding marinade (see Tip, below).

Thread pork onto skewers. Cook on a greased grill on medium for about 5 minutes per side until meat reaches desired doneness.

Grill pita breads for 1 to 2 minutes per side until heated through. Cut into 6 pieces each. Arrange on a serving plate with pork skewers.

Combine remaining 3 ingredients. Serve with pork skewers and pita. Serves 6.

1 serving: 230 Calories; 11 g Total Fat (6 g Mono, 1 g Poly, 2.5 g Sat); 40 mg Cholesterol; 19 g Carbohydrate (trace Fibre, 3 g Sugar); 16 g Protein; 320 mg Sodium

Tip: If you want to baste your skewers with any leftover marinade, boil it first to prevent any contamination from the raw meat. Never save and reuse uncooked marinade.

Candied Chicken Sticks

Maple syrup and Indonesian sweet soy sauce give these chicken skewers a delicious sweetness. Your guests will find the flavours familiar, yet somehow exotic and elusive.

Maple syrup	1/2 cup	125 mL
Chili garlic sauce	2 tbsp.	30 mL
Indonesian sweet soy sauce	2 tbsp.	30 mL
Boneless, skinless chicken breast halves, cut lengthwise into 1/4 inch (6 mm) thick slices	1/2 lb.	225 g
Bamboo skewers (8 inches, 20 cm, each), soaked in water for 10 minutes	8	8
Finely shredded suey choy (Chinese cabbage), lightly packed	2 cups	500 mL
Green onions, cut into 3 inch (7.5 cm) lengths	2	2
Rice vinegar	1 tbsp.	15 mL

Combine first 3 ingredients. Reserve 1/4 cup (60 mL) syrup mixture. Combine chicken and remaining syrup mixture in a medium resealable freezer bag. Marinate in refrigerator for at least 6 hours or overnight. Drain, discarding marinade.

Thread chicken onto skewers. Cook on a well-greased grill on medium for 1 to 2 minutes per side until chicken is glazed and no longer pink inside. Brush with 2 tbsp. (30 mL) reserved syrup mixture.

Toss cabbage and green onion together on a serving platter. Stir vinegar into remaining syrup mixture and drizzle over cabbage mixture. Top with skewers. Serves 4.

1 serving: 150 Calories; 1 g Total Fat (0 g Mono, 0 g Poly, 0 g Sat); 35 mg Cholesterol; 24 g Carbohydrate (trace Fibre, 22 g Sugar); 14 g Protein; 690 mg Sodium

Feta and Herb Eggplant Rolls

The rich royal purple skin of an Asian eggplant lends an intriguing hue to this sophisticated roll. The fresh flavours with smoky accents and a hint of tang are bound to tantalize.

Asian eggplants, ends trimmed	3	3
Olive oil	2 tbsp.	30 mL
Salt, sprinkle		
Pepper, sprinkle		
Canned roasted whole red peppers, drained, blotted dry, cut into 4 strips each	3	3
Crumbled feta cheese	1/2 cup	125 mL
Herb and garlic cream cheese	1/4 cup	60 mL
Chopped fresh basil	3 tbsp.	45 mL
Arugula leaves	36	36
Wooden cocktail picks	12	12
Balsamic vinegar	2 tbsp.	30 mL

Cut eggplants lengthwise into 6 slices each, about 1/4 inch (6 mm) thick. Discard outside slices. Brush both sides of slices with olive oil and sprinkle with salt and pepper. Cook on a greased grill on medium for about 5 minutes until browned. Let stand until cool.

Place 1 strip of red pepper on each eggplant slice.

Combine next 3 ingredients and spread over red pepper. Arrange arugula leaves over top. Roll up eggplant slices to enclose filling, securing with wooden picks. Arrange rolls, seam side down, on a serving plate.

Brush with vinegar. Serve at room temperature. Makes 12 rolls.

1 serving: 80 Calories; 4.5 g Total Fat (2 g Mono, 0 g Poly, 2 g Sat); 10 mg Cholesterol; 7 g Carbohydrate (3 g Fibre, 4 g Sugar); 2 g Protein; 170 mg Sodium

Curried Chicken Samosa Strudel

The crisp, delicate and flaky texture of phyllo pastry heightens the sensation of biting into these mildly spiced strudels.

Cooking oil	2 tsp.	10 mL
Minced onion	1 1/2 cups	375 mL
Madras curry paste	2 tbsp.	30 mL
Garlic cloves, minced	2	2
Canned chickpeas (garbanzo beans), rinsed and drained, mashed	1 cup	250 mL
Chopped cooked chicken breast	1 cup	250 mL
Frozen peas	1/2 cup	125 mL
Grated carrot	1/2 cup	125 mL
Phyllo pastry sheets, thawed according to package directions	8	8
Unsalted butter, melted	1/4 cup	60 mL

Heat cooking oil in a frying pan on medium. Add next 3 ingredients and cook until onion starts to soften. Let stand until cool.

Stir in next 4 ingredients.

Layer 4 sheets of phyllo pastry, lightly brushing each layer with melted butter. Keep remaining phyllo covered with a damp towel to prevent drying. Spread half of chicken mixture along bottom of sheet, leaving a 1 1/2 inch (3.8 cm) edge on each side. Fold in sides and roll up from bottom to enclose. Place, seam side down, on an ungreased baking sheet. Brush with butter. Cut several small vents on top to allow steam to escape. Repeat. Bake in a 400°F (200°C) oven for about 20 minutes until golden. With a serrated knife, cut strudels diagonally into 7 slices each. Makes 14 slices.

1 serving: 140 Calories; 5 g Total Fat (1.5 g Mono, 0 g Poly, 2.5 g Sat); 15 mg Cholesterol; 16 g Carbohydrate (2 g Fibre, 2 g Sugar); 7 g Protein; 170 mg Sodium

Shrimp Mango Summer Rolls with Cool Herbs and Chili Heat

A touch of chili heat mingles with the cool crispness of mint and cilantro in these rolls that are filled with everything light, cool and refreshing.

Rice vermicelli	2 oz.	57 g
Chopped fresh mint	2 tbsp.	30 mL
Lime juice	2 tbsp.	30 mL
Sweet chili sauce	2 tbsp.	30 mL
Fish sauce	2 tsp.	10 mL
Rice paper rounds (7 inch, 18 cm, diameter), (see How To, below)	6	6
Fresh cilantro leaves	12	12
Cooked medium shrimp (peeled and deveined), halved lengthwise	6	6
Mango slices, 1/8 inch (3 mm) thick (see Tip, below)	6	6

Cover vermicelli with boiling water. Let stand until just tender. Drain. Rinse with cold water, draining well.

Add next 4 ingredients and toss well.

Place 1 rice paper round in a shallow bowl of hot water until just softened (see How To, below). Place on a clean tea towel. Place 2 cilantro leaves in the centre of the rice paper and 2 shrimp halves over top. Cover with a mango slice. Spoon about 3 tbsp. (45 mL) vermicelli mixture over top. Fold in sides and roll up tightly from bottom to enclose. Repeat. Serve with sweet chili sauce. Makes 6 rolls.

1 serving: 120 Calories; 0.5 g Total Fat (0 g Mono, 0 g Poly, 0 g Sat); 35 mg Cholesterol; 22 g Carbohydrate (trace Fibre, 3 g Sugar); 5 g Protein; 260 mg Sodium

Tip: If fresh mango isn't available, drained, canned mango can be substituted. The texture will be softer but the overall taste won't be compromised.

HOW TO WORK WITH RICE PAPER

To become pliable, rice paper must be softened in water. Thicker rice paper (as used in this recipe) requires hotter water whereas the thinner varieties can be softened in cooler water. If working with hot water, make sure to change it as it cools. Always soften one sheet at a time, quickly and evenly. If the rice paper becomes too soft, it may become sticky and hard to work with.

Crispy Jerk Chicken Rolls

Indulge your guests with the crisp fried fare that is so enjoyed at get-togethers— just make yours a cut above the rest with the Jamaican flair of spicy jerk chicken.

Cooking oil	1 tsp.	5 mL
Chopped onion	1 cup	250 mL
Grated carrot	1 cup	250 mL
Chopped pickled jalapeño pepper	1 tbsp.	15 mL
Jerk paste	1 1/4 tsp.	6 mL
Garlic clove, minced	1	1
Ground allspice	1/8 tsp.	0.5 mL
Chopped cooked chicken	1 cup	250 mL
Plain yogurt	2 tbsp.	30 mL
Spring roll wrappers (6 inch, 15 cm, square)	8	8
Egg white (large)	1	1
Water	1 tbsp.	15 mL
Cooking oil	3 cups	750 mL

Heat cooking oil in a frying pan on medium. Add next 6 ingredients and cook for about 10 minutes until onion is softened.

Stir in chicken and yogurt.

Arrange wrappers on work surface. Place about 1/4 cup (60 mL) chicken mixture near bottom right corner. Fold corner up and over filling, folding in sides. In a small bowl, combine egg white and water, and dampen wrapper edges with mixture. Roll to opposite corner and press to seal. Repeat.

Heat cooking oil in a large frying pan on medium-high (see How To, page 63). Shallow-fry 2 or 3 rolls at a time, turning often, until golden. Transfer to a plate lined with paper towel. Makes 8 rolls.

1 serving: 160 Calories; 8 g Total Fat (4 g Mono, 2 g Poly, 1 g Sat); 45 mg Cholesterol; 16 g Carbohydrate (1 g Fibre, 2 g Sugar); 8 g Protein; 190 mg Sodium

Parmesan Cones with White Bean Mousse

They may look like a sweet treat, but these cones are rich and savoury. The interplay of Parmesan, basil and lemon is delightfully unexpected. Don't cheat yourself by using powdered Parmesan. Grate the fresh stuff for truly magnificent flavour and perfect results.

Grated fresh Parmesan cheese	3/4 cup	175 mL
Pepper	1/4 tsp.	1 mL
Canned white kidney beans, rinsed and drained	1 cup	250 mL
Basil pesto	1 tbsp.	15 mL
Lemon juice	2 tsp.	10 mL
Olive oil	2 tsp.	10 mL

Cut two 3 1/2 inch (9 cm) diameter circles from heavy paper. Shape into cones and tape or staple securely. Place a sheet of parchment paper on a baking sheet (see Tip, below). Trace two 3 1/2 inch (9 cm) diameter circles, about 3 inches (7.5 cm) apart. Turn paper over. Combine cheese and pepper and spread about 1 tbsp. (15 mL) cheese mixture over each circle. Bake in a 350°F (175°C) oven for about 5 minutes until melted and golden. Let stand for 1 minute. Transfer cheese round to a plate. Immediately place 1 paper cone on cheese and roll around cone. Repeat with second cheese round and cone. Let stand until cool. Wipe parchment paper to remove any crumbs. Repeat.

In a blender or food processor, process remaining 4 ingredients until smooth. Spoon into a small freezer bag with a small piece snipped off 1 corner. Pipe into cones. Serve immediately. Makes about 10 cones.

1 serving: 70 Calories; 4 g Total Fat (1.5 g Mono, 0 g Poly, 1.5 g Sat); 5 mg Cholesterol; 4 g Carbohydrate (2 g Fibre, 0 g Sugar); 4 g Protein; 160 mg Sodium

Tip: Have two separate baking sheets at the ready, each with their own parchment paper with circles drawn on, so you can put the second one in the oven while the first one cools.

Prosciutto Arugula Herb Wraps

Worlds collide with this French and Italian-inspired delicacy. Thin little pancakes are infused with herbs and wrapped around peppery arugula and salty prosciutto.

Milk	1 cup	250 mL
Large eggs	2	2
Butter, melted	1 1/2 tbsp.	25 mL
Chopped fresh basil	1 tbsp.	15 mL
Chopped fresh oregano	1 tbsp.	15 mL
Chopped fresh thyme	2 tsp.	10 mL
Salt	1/2 tsp.	2 mL
All-purpose flour	1/2 cup	125 mL
Cooking oil	1 tbsp.	15 mL
Chopped arugula leaves, lightly packed	1 1/2 cups	375 mL
Chopped prosciutto ham	2/3 cup	150 mL
Sour cream	1/3 cup	75 mL

In a blender or food processor, process first 7 ingredients. Transfer to a bowl. Whisk in flour until smooth.

Heat 1/4 tsp. (1 mL) cooking oil in a small frying pan on medium. Pour about 2 tbsp. (30 mL) batter into pan. Immediately tilt and swirl pan to ensure bottom is covered. Cook for about 1 minute until brown spots appear. Turn over. Cook until golden. Transfer to a plate. Repeat with remaining batter, adding and heating cooking oil between batches to prevent sticking.

Combine remaining 3 ingredients. Spoon about 2 tbsp. (30 mL) along centre of each wrapper. Fold in sides and roll up from bottom to enclose. Place, seam side down, on a serving plate. Makes about 12 rolls.

1 serving: 110 Calories; 7 g Total Fat (2 g Mono, 0.5 g Poly, 3 g Sat); 55 mg Cholesterol; 6 g Carbohydrate (0 g Fibre, 1 g Sugar); 7 g Protein; 390 mg Sodium

Seta Antojitos Especial

This tortilla wrap surprises. Madiera and portobello add a richness and body that completely satisfies.

Olive oil	1 tbsp.	15 mL
Chopped portobello mushrooms	4 cups	1 L
Chopped leek (white part only)	1/2 cup	125 mL
Salt	1/4 tsp.	1 mL
Pepper	1/4 tsp.	1 mL
Madeira	2 tbsp.	30 mL
Chopped fresh thyme	1 1/2 tsp.	7 mL
Grated havarti cheese	1 1/2 cups	375 mL
Flour tortillas (9 inch, 23 cm, diameter)	2	2

Heat olive oil in a large frying pan on medium-high. Add next 4 ingredients and cook until mushrooms are browned and liquid is evaporated.

Add Madeira and thyme and cook until wine is all evaporated. Remove from heat.

Stir in cheese. Spread over tortillas, leaving a 1/2 inch (12 mm) border. Roll up to enclose. Place, seam side down, on a greased baking sheet. Bake in a 400°F (200°C) oven until browned and cheese is melted. Let stand for 2 minutes. Trim ends and cut diagonally into 5 slices each. Makes 10 slices.

1 slice: 190 Calories; 14 g Total Fat (4 g Mono, 0 g Poly, 9 g Sat); 40 mg Cholesterol; 8 g Carbohydrate (trace Fibre, 1 g Sugar); 9 g Protein; 360 mg Sodium

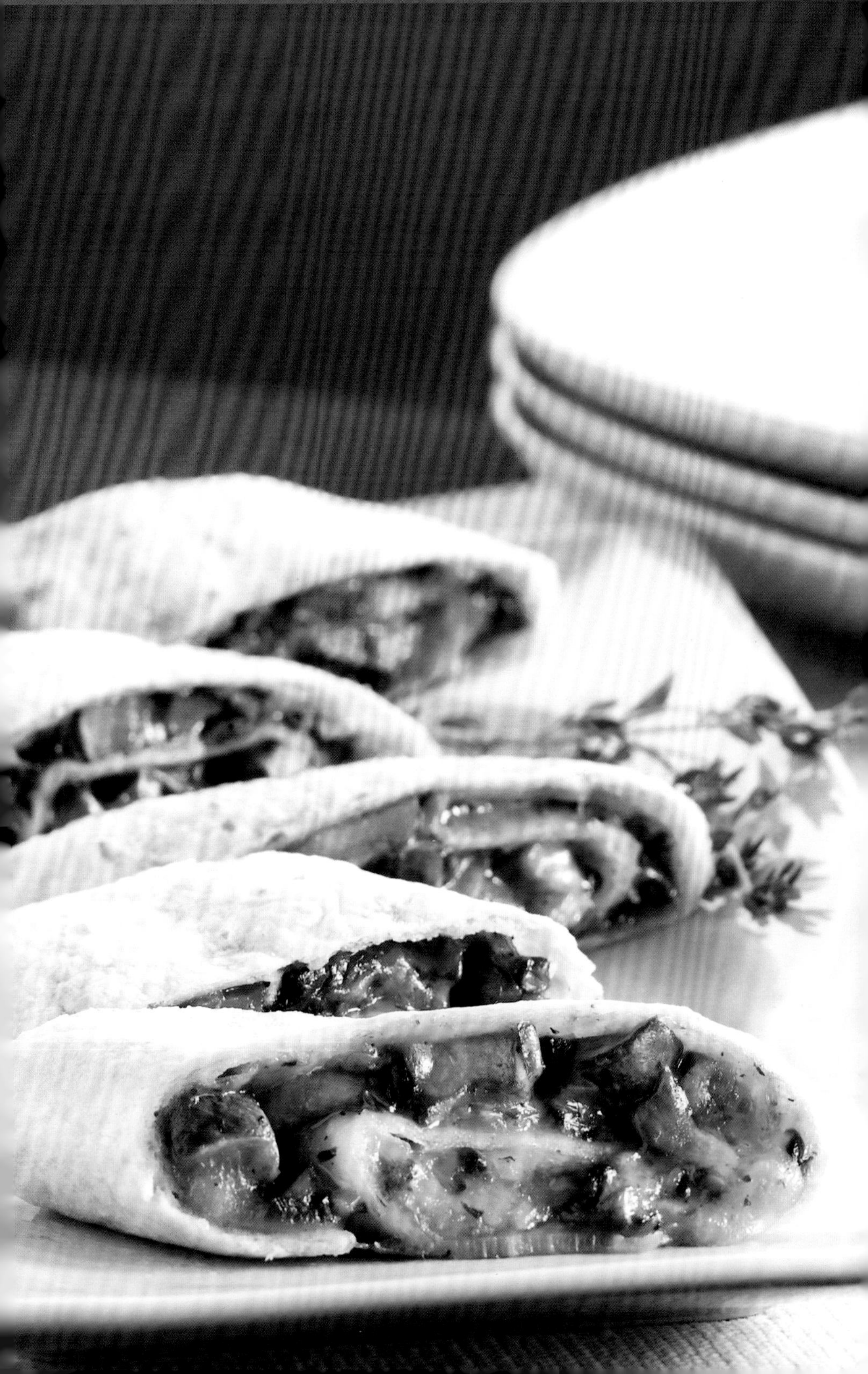

Smoked Salmon Rice Rolls

Smoked salmon adds extra dimension to this special salad roll. The rich, salty fish and the cool, fresh vegetables are balanced in Zen-like proportion.

Mixed baby greens	1 cup	250 mL
Julienned smoked salmon slices	6 oz.	170 g
(see How To, below)		
Julienned English cucumber	1/2 cup	125 mL
(see How To, below)		
Enoki mushrooms	3 oz.	85 g
Grated carrot	1/3 cup	75 mL
Julienned green onion	1/4 cup	60 mL
(see How To, below)		
Sprigs of fresh dill, stems removed	6	6
Rice paper rounds (9 inch, 23 cm, diameter)	6	6
Black sesame seeds	1 tsp.	5 mL
Ponzu sauce (see Tip, below)	1/3 cup	75 mL

Divide each of the first 7 ingredients into 6 equal portions.

Place 1 rice paper round in a shallow bowl of hot water until just softened (see How To, page 106). Place on a clean tea towel. Arrange 1 portion of filling along centre of rice paper. Fold in sides and roll up tightly from bottom to enclose. Place, seam side down, on a serving plate. Repeat.

Sprinkle sesame seeds over rolls. Serve with ponzu sauce. Makes 6 rolls.

1 serving: 110 Calories; 1.5 g Total Fat (0.5 g Mono, 0 g Poly, 0 g Sat); 5 mg Cholesterol; 15 g Carbohydrate (1 g Fibre, 3 g Sugar); 8 g Protein; 640 mg Sodium

Tip: If you can't find ponzu sauce, simply add a little lemon juice to regular soy sauce.

HOW TO JULIENNE

To julienne, cut into thin matchstick-like strips.

Creamy Wild Mushrooms on Pastry Points

A rich flavour and an elegant presentation. Sometimes the simplest things yield the most fantastic results.

14 oz. (397 g) package of puff pastry, thawed according to package directions	1/2	1/2
Butter	2 tbsp.	30 mL
Chopped fresh shiitake mushrooms	3 cups	750 mL
Chopped fresh oyster mushrooms	2 cups	500 mL
Finely chopped onion	1/3 cup	75 mL
Garlic clove, minced	1	1
Salt	1/4 tsp.	1 mL
Pepper	1/8 tsp.	0.5 mL
Dry sherry	3 tbsp.	45 mL
Chopped fresh thyme	1/2 tsp.	2 mL
Whipping cream	2/3 cup	150 mL

Roll out pastry to a 12 x 5 inch (30 x 12.5 cm) rectangle. Cut crosswise into 6 rectangles. Cut rectangles diagonally to form triangles and arrange on a baking sheet. Bake in a 400°F (200°C) oven for 15 to 20 minutes until golden. Let stand until cool.

Melt butter in a frying pan on medium-high. Add next 6 ingredients and cook for about 15 minutes until onion is soft and mushrooms are browned.

Stir in sherry, thyme and cream. Serve over pastry points. Serves 6.

1 serving: 330 Calories; 25 g Total Fat (11 g Mono, 2 g Poly, 11 g Sat); 40 mg Cholesterol; 20 g Carbohydrate (1 g Fibre, trace Sugar); 5 g Protein; 270 mg Sodium

Five-spiced Crepes with Coconut Scallops

An exotic and intriguing flavour experience. The scent of aromatic spices will give your guests just a hint of what they are about to enjoy.

Large egg	1	1
Milk	1/2 cup	125 mL
All-purpose flour	6 tbsp.	100 mL
Butter, melted	1 1/2 tbsp.	25 mL
Granulated sugar	1/2 tsp.	2 mL
Chinese five-spice powder	1/4 tsp.	1 mL
Cooking oil	1 1/2 tsp.	7 mL
Sesame oil	2 tsp.	10 mL
Coarsely chopped scallops	1 cup	250 mL
Chopped green onion	2 tbsp.	30 mL
Seasoned salt	1/2 tsp.	2 mL
Coconut milk	1/2 cup	125 mL
Cornstarch	1 tsp.	5 mL

Using a blender or food processor, process first 6 ingredients until smooth. Let stand for 30 minutes.

Heat 1/4 tsp. (1 mL) cooking oil in a small frying pan on medium. Pour about 2 tbsp. (30 mL) batter into pan. Immediately tilt and swirl pan to ensure bottom is covered. Cook for about 1 minute until brown spots appear. Transfer to a plate. Repeat with remaining batter, heating cooking oil between batches to prevent sticking. Fold crepes into quarters and arrange on a serving plate.

Heat sesame oil in the same frying pan on medium. Add next 3 ingredients and cook for 1 minute. Combine coconut milk and cornstarch and add to the pan. Heat and stir for about 1 minute until scallops are opaque and sauce is bubbling. Spoon over crepes. Serves 6.

1 serving: 160 Calories; 11 g Total Fat (3.5 g Mono, 2 g Poly, 4.5 g Sat); 55 mg Cholesterol; 5 g Carbohydrate (0 g Fibre, trace Sugar); 11 g Protein; 250 mg Sodium

Shrimp with Horseradish Beet Coulis

A feast for the eyes and the palate with strong, bold flavours and vibrant colours— perfect for a sophisticated get-together.

Uncooked extra-large shrimp (peeled and deveined)	12	12
Montreal steak spice	1 tsp.	5 mL
Olive oil	2 tsp.	10 mL
14 oz. (398 mL) can of whole baby beets, puréed with 3 tbsp. (45 mL) juice	1	1
Butter, melted	2 tbsp.	30 mL
Prepared horseradish	1 tbsp.	15 mL
Chopped fresh dill	2 tsp.	10 mL
Arugula leaves, lightly packed	1/4 cup	60 mL

Combine shrimp and steak spice. Let stand for 15 minutes. Heat olive oil in a frying pan on medium. Add shrimp and cook until pink.

Combine next 4 ingredients and pour onto a serving plate.

Arrange arugula and shrimp over top. Serves 4.

1 serving: 140 Calories; 8 g Total Fat (3 g Mono, 0.5 g Poly, 4 g Sat); 50 mg Cholesterol; 8 g Carbohydrate (2 g Fibre, 6 g Sugar); 9 g Protein; 650 mg Sodium

Coconut Chili Soup

Transport yourself to the tropics with this smooth, velvety soup. The intensity comes from Thai red curry paste—just enough to really heat things up.

Sesame oil	2 tsp.	10 mL
Finely chopped onion	1/2 cup	125 mL
Garlic clove, minced	1	1
Thai red curry paste	1/2 tsp.	2 mL
Coconut milk	1 cup	250 mL
Prepared vegetable broth	1/2 cup	125 mL
Brown sugar, packed	1 tsp.	5 mL
Soy sauce	1 tsp.	5 mL
Lime juice	3/4 tsp.	4 mL

Heat sesame oil in a saucepan on medium. Add next 3 ingredients and cook for about 5 minutes until onion is softened.

Stir in next 4 ingredients. Simmer, covered, for 10 minutes to blend flavours. Remove from heat.

Stir in lime juice. Using a hand blender, process until smooth (see Safety Tip, below). Strain into 4 small serving bowls and discard solids. Serves 4.

1 serving: 150 Calories; 14 g Total Fat (1.5 g Mono, 1 g Poly, 11 g Sat); 0 mg Cholesterol; 6 g Carbohydrate (0 g Fibre, 2 g Sugar); 2 g Protein; 180 mg Sodium

Safety Tip: We recommend that you not use a countertop blender to process hot liquids.

Smoked Salmon Blintz Cups

Blintzes are known for being labour-intensive, but we've found a great way to make them without all the fuss. Creamy smoked salmon filling hides inside a rich, golden batter for an unforgettable flavour.

Ricotta cheese	1/2 cup	125 mL
Chopped smoked salmon	1/4 cup	60 mL
Cream cheese, softened	1/4 cup	60 mL
Chopped fresh dill	1 tbsp.	15 mL
Pepper	1/4 tsp.	1 mL
All-purpose flour	1 cup	250 mL
Baking powder	1 tsp.	5 mL
Salt	1/4 tsp	1 mL
Large eggs	3	3
Milk	1/3 cup	75 mL
Butter, melted	2 tbsp.	30 mL
Granulated sugar	2 tbsp.	30 mL

Combine first 5 ingredients. Set aside.

Combine next 3 ingredients in a small bowl. Make a well in the centre.

Whisk next 4 ingredients in a separate bowl and add to the well. Whisk until smooth. Pour about 1/4 cup (60 mL) batter into each of 6 greased 6 oz. (170 mL) ramekins. Carefully spoon salmon mixture over batter. Pour remaining batter over top. Bake in a 350°F (175°C) oven for 15 to 18 minutes until slightly puffed but firm to the touch. Let stand for 5 minutes before removing blintz cups from ramekins to a serving plate. Makes 6 blintz cups.

1 serving: 230 Calories; 11 g Total Fat (2.5 g Mono, 0.5 g Poly, 6 g Sat); 130 mg Cholesterol; 23 g Carbohydrate (trace Fibre, 6 g Sugar); 10 g Protein; 340 mg Sodium

Almond Brie Croutons on Apple-dressed Spinach

This delicately dressed spinach salad is adorned with decadent "croutons"— crusted in almonds and featuring a soft Brie centre.

Large egg, fork-beaten	1	1
Maple syrup	1 tbsp.	15 mL
7 1/2 oz. (200 g) Brie cheese round, cut into 6 wedges (see Tip, below)	1	1
All-purpose flour	1/4 cup	60 mL
Finely chopped sliced natural almonds	1 cup	250 mL
Maple syrup	2 tbsp.	30 mL
Olive oil	2 tbsp.	30 mL
White balsamic (or wine) vinegar	2 tbsp.	30 mL
Fresh spinach leaves, lightly packed	1 1/2 cups	375 mL
Unpeeled green apple, core removed and cut crosswise into thin rings	1	1

Combine egg and first amount of maple syrup.

Press cheese wedges into flour until coated. Dip into egg mixture, then press firmly into almonds until coated. Freeze for 45 minutes. Place wedges on a baking sheet. Bake in a 450°F (230°C) oven for about 7 minutes until almonds start to brown on edges and cheese starts to soften.

Combine next 3 ingredients in a bowl. Add spinach and apple and toss until coated. Spoon onto a serving plate, placing some of the apple rings over spinach. Arrange cheese wedges over top. Serves 6.

1 serving: 310 Calories; 22 g Total Fat (11 g Mono, 3 g Poly, 7 g Sat); 70 mg Cholesterol; 17 g Carbohydrate (3 g Fibre, 9 g Sugar); 12 g Protein; 230 mg Sodium

Tip: When working with softer cheeses such as Brie, you can freeze them for 15 to 20 minutes to make cutting and portioning easier.

Sun-dried Tomato and Leek Mussels

Plump, juicy mussels bathe in a pesto, wine and leek sauce. Serve with crusty French bread for dipping.

Mussels (see Note, below)	1 lb.	454 g
Olive oil	1 1/2 tsp.	7 mL
Finely chopped leek (white part only)	1/2 cup	125 mL
Garlic clove, minced	1	1
Dried crushed chilies	1/8 tsp.	0.5 mL
Dry white wine	3/4 cup	175 mL
Sun-dried tomato pesto	2 tbsp.	30 mL

Lightly tap to close any mussels that are opened 1/4 inch (6 mm) or more. Discard any that do not close.

Heat olive oil in a saucepan on medium. Add next 3 ingredients and cook for about 5 minutes until leek is softened.

Stir in wine and pesto. Bring to a boil and add mussels. Cook, covered, for about 5 minutes until mussels are opened. Discard any unopened mussels. Serves 4.

1 serving: 180 Calories; 7 g Total Fat (2 g Mono, 1 g Poly, 1 g Sat); 30 mg Cholesterol; 8 g Carbohydrate (trace Fibre, 1 g Sugar); 14 g Protein; 370 mg Sodium

Note: For safety reasons, it is important to discard any mussels that do not close before cooking, as well as any that have not opened during cooking. Mussels must be still alive when you cook them. If you tap them before cooking and they don't close, they are dead; similarly if they don't open when being cooked, they were dead before being cooked and are not safe to eat.

Mango Gazpacho

A cool, upbeat take on gazpacho. Mango is the hero in this chilled soup with cilantro as the sidekick. There's something distinctively modern about the pairing of these two flavours.

Chopped mango (see Tip, below)	1 cup	250 mL
Orange juice	1/3 cup	75 mL
Chopped fresh cilantro	1 tbsp.	15 mL
Lime juice	1 tbsp.	15 mL
Brown sugar, packed	1/2 tsp.	2 mL
Finely grated ginger root	1/2 tsp.	2 mL
Ground cumin	1/2 tsp.	2 mL
Salt	1/2 tsp.	2 mL
Pepper	1/8 tsp.	0.5 mL
Diced English cucumber (with peel)	1/4 cup	60 mL
Diced mango	1/4 cup	60 mL
Diced red pepper	1/4 cup	60 mL

In a blender or food processor, process first 9 ingredients until smooth.

Stir in remaining 3 ingredients. Chill, covered, for about 1 hour until cold. Pour into 4 small serving cups. Serves 4.

1 serving: 50 Calories; 0 g Total Fat (0 g Mono, 0 g Poly, 0 g Sat); 0 mg Cholesterol; 13 g Carbohydrate (1 g Fibre, 9 g Sugar); trace Protein; 290 mg Sodium

Tip: For faster prep, use frozen mango. Chop it up while it's still icy and you'll save time on the chill factor.

Miso Mushroom Risotto with Scallops

Asian flavours of sesame and miso meet Italian risotto for an intriguing union of cultural cookery.

Sesame oil	2 tsp.	10 mL
Chopped fresh shiitake mushrooms	2 cups	500 mL
Chopped green onion	1/4 cup	60 mL
Dry white wine	1/3 cup	75 mL
White miso	1 tbsp.	15 mL
Arborio rice	1/2 cup	125 mL
Water	1 1/3 cups	325 mL
Salt	1/2 tsp.	2 mL
Sesame oil	2 tsp.	10 mL
Large sea scallops	4	4
Sea salt	1/2 tsp.	2 mL

Heat first amount of sesame oil in a saucepan on medium. Add mushrooms and green onion and cook for about 8 minutes until mushrooms are browned.

Stir in wine and miso and cook until wine is almost all evaporated. Add rice and stir for 30 seconds.

Stir in water and salt. Bring to a boil. Simmer, covered, on medium-low for about 20 minutes, without stirring, until rice is tender. Let stand, covered, for 5 minutes.

Heat second amount of sesame oil in a frying pan on medium. Add scallops, sprinkle with sea salt and cook for about 3 minutes until scallops are opaque and browned. Stir risotto and divide into 4 small bowls, placing 1 scallop over top. Serves 4.

1 serving: 190 Calories; 4.5 g Total Fat (2 g Mono, 2 g Poly, 0.5 g Sat); 10 mg Cholesterol; 24 g Carbohydrate (1 g Fibre, trace Sugar); 8 g Protein; 770 mg Sodium

Seared Scallops Verde

An unpredicted pairing of succulent chili-crusted scallops with the tang of a tomatillo salsa is made even more exceptional with the addition of fresh watermelon.

Lime juice	3 tbsp.	45 mL
Olive oil	2 tbsp.	30 mL
Salt	1/8 tsp.	0.5 mL
Pepper	1/8 tsp.	0.5 mL
Large sea scallops	8	8
Chili powder, sprinkle		
Olive oil	1 tbsp.	15 mL
Tomatillo salsa (or salsa verde)	1/2 cup	125 mL
Small seedless watermelon triangles, about 1/2 inch (12 mm) thick	8	8

Combine first 4 ingredients. Add scallops and stir. Marinate for 15 minutes. Drain, discarding marinade.

Sprinkle chili powder over scallops. Heat second amount of olive oil in a frying pan on medium-high. Add scallops and sear for about 1 minute per side until scallops are just opaque.

Spoon small portions of salsa onto 8 small plates. Place watermelon triangles over salsa. Place scallops over watermelon and top with remaining salsa. Serves 8.

1 serving: 80 Calories; 5 g Total Fat (3.5 g Mono, 0.5 g Poly, 0.5 g Sat); trace Cholesterol; 5 g Carbohydrate (0 g Fibre, 0 g Sugar); 3 g Protein; 130 mg Sodium

Praline Pecans, Beets and Blue Cheese on Baby Greens

Vivid beet and candied pecans add a distinguished essence to blue cheese and mixed greens. With the addition of a citrus and Dijon dressing, the result is a virtual kaleidoscope of flavours.

Medium fresh beet, scrubbed clean	1	1
Butter	2 tsp.	10 mL
Brown sugar, lightly packed	1/4 cup	60 mL
Pecan halves	3/4 cup	175 mL
Orange juice	1/4 cup	60 mL
Chopped fresh chives	2 tbsp.	30 mL
Olive oil	2 tbsp.	30 mL
White wine vinegar	2 tbsp.	30 mL
Dijon mustard	1 tbsp.	15 mL
Pepper	1/8 tsp.	0.5 mL
Mixed baby greens, lightly packed	1 1/2 cups	375 mL
Crumbled blue (or goat) cheese	1/2 cup	125 mL

Microwave beet, covered, for about 4 minutes until tender. Let stand until cool. Peel and cut into 1/4 inch (6 mm) wedges (see Tip, below).

Heat and stir butter and brown sugar in a frying pan until sugar is dissolved. Stir in pecans. Spread on a baking sheet lined with greased foil. Bake in a 375°F (190°C) oven for about 8 minutes, stirring once, until browned. Transfer to cutting board. Let stand until cool, then chop.

Whisk next 6 ingredients together.

Arrange greens in centre of a serving plate. Arrange beet wedges around greens. Sprinkle with cheese and pecans and drizzle with dressing. Serves 4.

1 serving: 350 Calories; 28 g Total Fat (15 g Mono, 5 g Poly, 7 g Sat); 20 mg Cholesterol; 21 g Carbohydrate (3 g Fibre, 16 g Sugar); 6 g Protein; 330 mg Sodium

Tip: Wear gloves when cutting fresh beets to avoid staining your hands. It is also easier to peel beets after they have been microwaved or roasted—the skins will slip off quite easily.

Shrimp Bisque

Elegant and rich-tasting bisque is most satisfying when sampled in small portions. These little bowls truly taste like traditional bisque, but take much less time to prepare.

Butter	1 tbsp.	15 mL
Uncooked medium shrimp (peeled and deveined), tails intact	6	6
Finely chopped celery	1/4 cup	60 mL
Finely chopped shallots	1/4 cup	60 mL
Uncooked shrimp (peeled and deveined), chopped	3 oz.	85 g
7 1/2 oz. (213 mL) can of tomato sauce	1	1
Whipping cream	1/3 cup	75 mL
Dry white wine	1/4 cup	60 mL
Chopped fresh tarragon	1/2 tsp.	2 mL
Fresh tarragon leaves	6	6

Melt butter in a saucepan on medium. Add first amount of shrimp and cook until pink. Transfer to a plate and set aside.

Add celery and shallots to the same saucepan and cook for about 5 minutes until softened.

Stir in next 5 ingredients. Simmer, covered, on medium-low for 5 minutes. Using a hand blender, process until smooth (see Safety Tip, below). Pour into 6 small serving cups.

Place 1 shrimp and 1 tarragon leaf over each cup of soup. Serves 6.

1 serving: 110 Calories; 6 g Total Fat (2 g Mono, 0 g Poly, 4 g Sat); 50 mg Cholesterol; 6 g Carbohydrate (0 g Fibre, 2 g Sugar); 5 g Protein; 260 mg Sodium

Safety Tip: We recommend that you not use a countertop blender to process hot liquids.

Coconut Lime Chicken Salad Cocktails

This inspired salad cocktail delivers the flavours of the tropics presented in a most unconventional manner. Whimsical in presentation but seriously delectable in taste.

Coconut milk	1/2 cup	125 mL
Brown sugar, packed	1 tbsp.	15 mL
Lime juice	1 tbsp.	15 mL
Dried crushed chilies	1/2 tsp.	2 mL
Seasoned salt	1/2 tsp.	2 mL
Thinly sliced cooked chicken	1 1/3 cups	325 mL
Julienned carrot (see How To, page 116)	1/2 cup	125 mL
Thinly sliced red pepper, about 2 inch (5 cm) long slices	1/2 cup	125 mL
Arugula leaves, lightly packed	2 cups	500 mL

Whisk first 5 ingredients together until sugar is dissolved. Add next 3 ingredients and toss. Chill, covered, for 1 to 2 hours.

Arrange arugula in 6 martini or cocktail glasses. Spoon chicken mixture over top. Serves 6.

1 serving: 110 Calories; 6 g Total Fat (1 g Mono, 0.5 g Poly, 4 g Sat); 30 mg Cholesterol; 4 g Carbohydrate (0 g Fibre, 3 g Sugar); 10 g Protein; 160 mg Sodium

Miso-glazed Cod on Ginger-spiked Cucumbers

Caramel-coloured glazed cod is set atop an Asian cucumber salad. The outcome is stylishly fresh and stimulating.

Paper-thin sliced English cucumber	2 cups	500 mL
Paper-thin red onion slice, halved and separated	1	1
Brown sugar, packed	2 tbsp.	30 mL
Mirin	2 tbsp.	30 mL
Rice vinegar	2 tbsp.	30 mL
Finely grated ginger root	1 tsp.	5 mL
Black sesame seeds	1 tsp.	5 mL
Sesame seeds	1 tsp.	5 mL
6 oz. (170 g) cod fillets, any small bones removed	2	2
Brown sugar, packed	3 tbsp.	45 mL
Mirin	3 tbsp.	45 mL
White miso	2 tbsp.	30 mL

Combine first 6 ingredients and marinate in refrigerator for 1 hour. Drain, discarding marinade. Arrange on a serving plate.

Sprinkle with sesame seeds.

Place cod fillets on a baking sheet. Microwave next 3 ingredients until brown sugar is dissolved and brush over fillets. Broil for 5 to 10 minutes until fish flakes easily when tested with a fork. Serve over cucumbers. Serves 4.

1 serving: 230 Calories; 1.5 g Total Fat (0 g Mono, 1 g Poly, 0 g Sat); 35 mg Cholesterol; 38 g Carbohydrate (1 g Fibre, 31 g Sugar); 17 g Protein; 520 mg Sodium

Citrus-glazed Lobster and Fennel

A simple dressing of orange reduction brings out the natural sweetness of the lobster. This dish will impress those guests with even the most adventurous palates.

Orange juice	1 cup	250 mL
Granulated sugar	2 tbsp.	30 mL
Sesame oil	2 tsp.	10 mL
Thinly sliced fennel bulb (white part only)	2 cups	500 mL
Garlic cloves, minced	2	2
Poppy seeds, sprinkle		
Sesame oil	2 tsp.	10 mL
Raw lobster tails, meat removed (see How To, below), cut into 6 pieces each	2	2
Sea salt, sprinkle		

Combine orange juice and sugar in a saucepan. Boil gently on medium for about 20 minutes, stirring occasionally, until reduced to about 1/4 cup (60 mL).

Heat first amount of sesame oil in a frying pan on medium. Add fennel and garlic and cook for about 5 minutes until fennel is tender-crisp. Transfer to a serving plate.

Drizzle with 1 tbsp. (15 mL) juice reduction and sprinkle with poppy seeds.

Heat second amount of sesame oil. Add lobster and sprinkle with sea salt. Cook for about 3 minutes until lobster is opaque and lightly browned. Arrange over fennel, drizzling with remaining juice reduction. Serves 4.

1 serving: 170 Calories; 5 g Total Fat (2 g Mono, 2 g Poly, 1 g Sat); 70 mg Cholesterol; 17 g Carbohydrate (2 g Fibre, 6 g Sugar); 14 g Protein; 230 mg Sodium

HOW TO REMOVE LOBSTER MEAT

To remove the lobster meat from the tail, firmly grasp the tail and snap off the flipper portion. Use a fork to press up from the flipper end and push the meat out of the top of the shell.

Chipotle Corn Soup

Chilled and velvety smooth yet contrasted with an intense, smoky chipotle pepper heat, this southwestern-influenced soup refreshes and invigorates all at once.

Butter	1 tsp.	5 mL
Chopped onion	1/2 cup	125 mL
Chopped chipotle pepper in adobo sauce (see Tip, below)	1 1/2 tsp.	7 mL
Prepared vegetable broth	1 1/2 cups	375 mL
Frozen kernel corn	1 1/2 cups	375 mL
Half-and-half cream	1/4 cup	60 mL
Salt	1/8 tsp.	0.5 mL

Melt butter in a saucepan on medium. Add onion and chipotle pepper and cook until onion is soft.

Add broth and corn. Simmer for about 10 minutes until corn is softened. Using a hand blender, process until smooth (see Safety Tip, page 124). Strain through a sieve, pressing solids with the back of a spoon. Discard solids.

Stir in cream and salt. Chill for about 4 hours until cold. Serves 4.

1 serving: 90 Calories; 4.5 g Total Fat (1 g Mono, 0 g Poly, 1.5 g Sat); 10 mg Cholesterol; 14 g Carbohydrate (2 g Fibre, 3 g Sugar); 2 g Protein; 310 mg Sodium

Tip: Store any leftover chipotle peppers in an airtight container in the fridge.

Chili Squid on Peas and Peppers

One of the joys of cooking is boldly stepping into new culinary territory, buying and preparing unfamiliar ingredients. Easily managed, this spicy squid delivers beautiful results.

Squid tubes (about 4 inches, 10 cm, each)	6	6
Soy sauce	1 tbsp.	15 mL
Dried crushed chilies	1/2 tsp.	2 mL
Cooking oil	2 tsp.	10 mL
Thinly sliced red pepper	1 cup	250 mL
Sugar snap peas	1/2 lb.	225 g
Garlic cloves, minced	2	2
Sweet chili sauce	1/3 cup	75 mL
Chili paste (sambal oelek)	1/4 tsp.	1 mL
Seasoned salt	1/2 tsp.	2 mL
Cooking oil	2 tsp.	10 mL

Cut squid tubes lengthwise to open flat. Score inside surface in a crosshatch pattern. Cut each piece in half and transfer to a bowl. Add soy sauce and chilies and stir. Chill, covered, for 30 minutes.

Heat a frying pan on medium-high until very hot. Add cooking oil. Add next 3 ingredients and stir-fry for about 1 minute until fragrant.

Add next 3 ingredients and stir-fry for about 2 minutes until vegetables are tender-crisp. Transfer to a serving plate.

Add second amount of cooking oil to the same frying pan. Add squid mixture and stir-fry for about 1 minute until squid curls. Arrange over vegetables, drizzling with pan juices. Serves 4.

1 serving: 140 Calories; 6 g Total Fat (3 g Mono, 1.5 g Poly, 6 g Sat); 70 mg Cholesterol; 16 g Carbohydrate (2 g Fibre, 11 g Sugar); 7 g Protein; 580 mg Sodium

Crisp Cinnamon Banana Boats

There's something alluring about the combination of bananas and caramel. Maybe it's the silky smoothness, maybe the sweetness. Whatever the appeal, it's nothing less than heavenly.

Small bananas, peeled and trimmed to 4 inches (10 cm) each	4	4
Flour tortillas (6 inch, 15 cm, diameter)	4	4
Granulated sugar	1/4 cup	60 mL
Ground cinnamon	2 tsp.	10 mL
Butter, melted	1/4 cup	60 mL
Caramel Irish cream liqueur	3 tbsp.	45 mL
Chocolate hazelnut spread	3 tbsp.	45 mL
Caramel (or butterscotch) ice cream topping	2/3 cup	150 mL

Place 1 banana on each tortilla. Fold in sides and roll up tightly from bottom to enclose. Secure with wooden picks (see How To, below).

Combine sugar and cinnamon in a shallow bowl.

Brush tortilla with melted butter and roll in cinnamon sugar. Place on a baking sheet. Bake in a 450°F (230°C) oven for about 8 minutes until golden. Cut in half diagonally.

Whisk liqueur and chocolate spread together until smooth. Drizzle onto a serving plate. Drizzle with ice cream topping. Arrange rolls over top. Serves 8.

1 serving: 260 Calories; 9 g Total Fat (2.5 g Mono, 0.5 g Poly, 4.5 g Sat); 15 mg Cholesterol; 43 g Carbohydrate (2 g Fibre, 14 g Sugar); 2 g Protein; 230 mg Sodium

HOW TO ROLL TORTILLAS

Fold in the sides of the tortilla and roll it up from the bottom. Push wooden picks through the wrapped tortilla to secure.

Cappuccino Meringue Stack

Melt-in-your-mouth meringue is given a twist with the addition of coffee, chocolate and just a hint of cinnamon. It's light on the palate, but certainly gets top grades for its refined flavour.

Icing (confectioner's) sugar	2 tbsp.	30 mL
Instant coffee granules, crushed to a fine powder	2 tsp.	10 mL
Cornstarch	1 1/2 tsp.	7 mL
Skim milk powder	1 1/2 tsp.	7 mL
Ground cinnamon, pinch		
Egg whites (large), room temperature	2	2
Brown sugar, packed	2 tbsp.	30 mL
Vanilla extract	1/2 tsp.	2 mL
Semi-sweet chocolate baking square (1 oz., 28 g), chopped	1	1

Combine first 5 ingredients.

Beat egg whites until soft peaks form (see How To, page 38). Gradually add brown sugar, beating until stiff peaks form. Fold in vanilla and coffee mixture. Spoon into a large freezer bag with a piece snipped off 1 corner. Pipe onto a parchment paper-lined baking sheet in a spiral pattern, leaving a 1/2 inch (12 mm) space between each round (see How To, below). Bake in a 250°F (120°C) oven for 1 1/2 hours. Let stand on baking sheet set on a wire rack until cool. Break into pieces and stack on a large plate.

Microwave chocolate on medium (50%) for about 1 minute, stirring every 15 seconds, until almost melted. Stir until smooth. Drizzle over meringue stack. Serves 6.

1 serving: 60 Calories; 1.5 g Total Fat (0 g Mono, 0 g Poly, 1 g Sat); 0 mg Cholesterol; 10 g Carbohydrate (0 g Fibre, 9 g Sugar); 2 g Protein; 23 mg Sodium

HOW TO PIPE AND BREAK MERINGUE

Pipe a spiral shape onto parchment paper, leaving a 1/2 inch (12 mm) space between the rounds. Break cooled meringue into large pieces.

Raspberry Crème Brûlée

Raspberry, chocolate and whipping cream topped with a crisp, sugary crust.
Simple preparation, yet this dessert is truly decadent.

Seedless raspberry jam	1/3 cup	75 mL
Raspberry liqueur	1 tbsp.	15 mL
Whipping cream	1 1/2 cups	375 mL
White chocolate baking squares (1 oz., 28 g, each), chopped	4	4
Egg yolks (large)	4	4
Granulated sugar	2 tbsp.	30 mL
Raspberry liqueur	1 tbsp.	15 mL
Granulated sugar	1/4 cup	60 mL

Place 4 greased 6 oz. (175 mL) ramekins in a 9 x 9 inch (23 x 23 cm) baking pan. Whisk jam and liqueur together until smooth. Spoon into ramekins and chill for about 30 minutes until firm.

Heat cream in a saucepan on medium until bubbles form around edge of pan. Remove from heat. Add chocolate and stir until melted.

Whisk next 3 ingredients together. Gradually whisk into cream mixture. Carefully pour into ramekins (see How To, below). Pour boiling water into pan until water comes halfway up sides of ramekins. Bake in a 300°F (150°C) oven for about 50 minutes until centres only wobble slightly. Transfer ramekins to a wire rack to cool completely. Chill, covered, for at least 6 hours or overnight.

Sprinkle 1 tbsp. (15 mL) sugar over each. Broil for about 5 minutes until sugar is browned and bubbling. Let stand for 5 minutes before serving. Makes 4 crème brûlées.

1 serving: 620 Calories; 42 g Total Fat (10 g Mono, 1.5 g Poly, 25 g Sat); 320 mg Cholesterol; 56 g Carbohydrate (0 g Fibre, 51 g Sugar); 6 g Protein; 60 mg Sodium

HOW TO POUR CUSTARD INTO RAMEKINS

To avoid disturbing the jam layer, carefully pour the custard over the back of a spoon.

Caramel Rum S'Mores

Brownies topped with ooey, gooey marshmallows, broiled and served with a rum caramel sauce for dipping. Sure to bring back memories of roasting marshmallows over a campfire.

Large marshmallows	6	6
Caramels	6	6
Whipping cream	1/4 cup	60 mL
Spiced rum	2 tbsp.	30 mL
Vanilla extract	1/2 tsp.	2 mL
Large marshmallows	8	8
Two-bite brownies	8	8
Cocktail picks or bamboo skewers	8	8

Microwave first 5 ingredients in a deep bowl (see Tip, below) on medium (50%) for about 5 minutes, stirring every 60 seconds, until almost melted. Stir until smooth. Cover to keep warm.

On a baking sheet, place 1 marshmallow over each brownie. Broil for about 1 minute until marshmallows are golden.

Push skewers through top of marshmallows and into brownies. Drizzle with caramel sauce. Makes 8 s'mores.

1 s'more: 160 Calories; 3 g Total Fat (1 g Mono, 0 g Poly, 0 g Sat); 20 mg Cholesterol; 23 g Carbohydrate (trace Fibre, 17 g Sugar); 2 g Protein; 60 mg Sodium

Tip: Because marshmallows expand when microwaved, be sure to use a large, deep bowl when heating the marshmallows for the caramel sauce. If you prefer, use a double boiler instead and make the sauce on the stovetop.

Lavalicious Chocolate Kisses

Decadent little chocolate bites with molten centres—this is one kiss you won't soon forget.

1 oz. (28 g) bittersweet chocolate baking square, chopped	1	1
1 oz. (28 g) semi-sweet chocolate baking square, chopped	1	1
Butter	1/4 cup	60 mL
Large eggs	2	2
Icing (confectioner's) sugar	2/3 cup	150 mL
Vanilla extract	1 tsp.	5 mL
All-purpose flour	1/4 cup	60 mL

Heat first 3 ingredients in a saucepan on lowest heat, stirring often, until chocolate is almost melted. Remove from heat. Stir until smooth. Let stand for 10 minutes.

Whisk next 3 ingredients together. Stir in chocolate mixture until combined.

Stir in flour until just moistened. Spoon into a small freezer bag with a small piece snipped off 1 corner. Fill 12 greased 1 oz. (30 mL) ramekins 3/4 full. Bake in a 425°F (220°C) oven for about 6 minutes until edges are set but centres still look wet and wobble slightly. Makes 12 kisses.

1 kiss: 100 Calories; 6 g Total Fat (1.5 g Mono, 0 g Poly, 3.5 g Sat); 45 mg Cholesterol; 10 g Carbohydrate (0 g Fibre, 7 g Sugar); 2 g Protein; 40 mg Sodium

Strawberry Mascarpone Trifles

Mascarpone cheese, strawberries, raspberry liqueur and light, sweet ladyfingers make this small sweet pure perfection.

Ladyfingers (about 4 inches, 10 cm, each)	6	6
15 oz. (425 g) container of frozen strawberries in light syrup, thawed	1	1
Raspberry liqueur	2 tbsp.	30 mL
Mascarpone cheese	1 1/4 cups	300 mL
Icing (confectioner's) sugar	1/3 cup	75 mL

Break 1 ladyfinger into pieces and place in 1 cocktail glass or dessert dish. Repeat with remaining ladyfingers, using a separate glass for each.

In a blender or food processor, process strawberries and liqueur until smooth. Pour over ladyfingers, reserving a small amount for topping.

Combine cheese and icing sugar. Spoon into a small freezer bag and snip a small piece off 1 corner. Pipe over strawberry mixture and drizzle with remaining strawberry mixture. Makes 6 trifles.

1 trifle: 430 Calories; 28 g Total Fat (0.5 g Mono, 0 g Poly, 20 g Sat); 155 mg Cholesterol; 35 g Carbohydrate (2 g Fibre, 28 Sugar); 6 g Protein; 45 mg Sodium

Ginger-poached Pears

Ultra-sweet icewine is the perfect ingredient for poaching pears. Paired with ginger and lemon, it's one hot ticket to a higher level of taste.

Small, firm peeled pears	4	4
Water	3 cups	750 mL
Icewine	1 cup	250 mL
Granulated sugar	1/2 cup	125 mL
Lemon juice	2 tbsp.	30 mL
Piece of ginger root (1 inch, 2.5 cm, length), chopped	1	1

Core pears from the bottom, leaving stems intact. Cut a thin slice from bottoms so pears will stand upright.

Combine remaining 5 ingredients in a large saucepan. Bring to a boil, stirring to dissolve sugar. Reduce heat to medium-low. Lay pears on their sides in pan. Simmer, covered, for 20 to 25 minutes, turning occasionally, until pears are tender when pierced with a knife. Transfer pears to a serving dish, using a slotted spoon. Remove and discard ginger. Boil poaching liquid on medium-high for about 20 minutes until reduced and slightly thickened. Serve with pears (see How To, below). Serves 4.

1 serving: 250 Calories; 0 g Total Fat (0 g Mono, 0 g Poly, 0 g Sat); 0 mg Cholesterol; 52 g Carbohydrate (5 g Fibre, 41 g Sugar); trace Protein; 5 mg Sodium

HOW TO SLICE PEARS FOR A FLOWER PETAL APPEARANCE

To cut your pears into a flower shape, make several cuts around the pear, starting about halfway up and cutting through to the bottom. Cut just to the centre of the pear, where the core has been removed.

Once you have made cuts all around the pear, gently spread out to make a flower shape.

Vanillacotta with Liqueur

When you get something as sinfully rich as this, you'll want it to last forever. Vanilla mingles with the slight tang of yogurt to provide perfect balance.

Unflavoured gelatin	4 tsp.	20 mL
Cold water	3 tbsp.	45 mL
Whipping cream	1/2 cup	125 mL
1/4 oz. (9 g) packet of vanilla sugar	1	1
Vanilla-bean flavoured yogurt (not fat-free)	1 cup	250 mL
Vanilla (or hazelnut) liqueur	1/2 cup	125 mL

Sprinkle gelatin over cold water in a saucepan. Let stand for 1 minute. Add cream and vanilla sugar. Heat and stir until sugar is dissolved. Remove from heat.

Whisk in yogurt until combined. Pour into 6 small glasses. Chill, covered, for at least 6 hours or overnight.

Pour liqueur over vanillacottas. Serves 6.

1 serving: 160 Calories; 8 g Total Fat (2 g Mono, 0 g Poly, 4.5 g Sat); 30 mg Cholesterol; 10 g Carbohydrate (0 g Fibre, 9 g Sugar); 2 g Protein; 45 mg Sodium

Lemon Thyme Sorbet

Citrus sorbet makes a great palate cleanser when there are lots of different flavours vying for your attention. A sorbet shooter is just enough to refresh the palate between appetizers.

Thin lemon slices	4	4
Water	1/2 cup	125 mL
Granulated sugar	3 tbsp.	45 mL
Sprigs of fresh thyme	2	2
Lemon juice	2 tbsp.	30 mL
Grated lemon zest	1/2 tsp.	2 mL
Finely chopped fresh thyme	1/2 tsp.	2 mL

Press lemon slices into 4 shot glasses and freeze.

Combine next 3 ingredients in a saucepan. Boil gently on medium for about 8 minutes. Remove and discard thyme sprigs.

Stir in remaining 3 ingredients. Let stand until slightly cooled. Pour into prepared shot glasses. Freeze for about 2 hours until firm. Serves 4.

1 serving: 35 Calories; 0 g Total Fat (0 g Mono, 0 g Poly, 0 g Sat); 0 mg Cholesterol; 10 g Carbohydrate (0 g Fibre, 9 g Sugar); 0 g Protein; 0 mg Sodium

Cocktails

A fantastic cocktail gets your guests in the mood for socializing and sets the tone for the evening. Whether it be a simple, classic martini or an elaborate and colourful cocktail, this will be the first taste your guests enjoy.

Here are a few favourites to try, each with a modern twist on tradition.

BLUE LAGOON

Pour 1 part white (light) rum, 1/2 part lychee liqueur and 2 parts orange juice over ice in a chilled cocktail glass. Add 1 tsp. (5 mL) lemon juice and top with club soda. Drizzle with 1 part blue-coloured, bitter orange liqueur and allow it to settle to the bottom.

CANADIAN SNOWBIRD

Pour 1 part Canadian whisky (rye), 4 parts apple juice and 1/2 part each of peach schnapps, lemon liqueur and maple syrup over ice in a chilled cocktail glass. Squeeze a lemon wedge over top and drop in.

BUENO BEER MARGARITAS

In a pitcher, combine a 12 oz. (341 mL) can of limeade concentrate with equal parts water, beer and tequila. Add 1/4 cup (60 mL) orange liqueur. Serve over crushed ice in margarita glasses.

ORANGE TRUFFLETINI

Combine 1 part vanilla vodka, 1 part chocolate liqueur and 1/2 part orange liqueur in a martini glass.

MOJITOS

Using a wooden spoon, crush or "muddle" 3 cut-up limes with 40 mint leaves and 1/4 cup (60 mL) granulated sugar in a 1 quart (1 L) pitcher. Add 1/4 cup (60 mL) lime cordial, if desired, to make a sweeter cocktail. Stir in 6 oz. (170 mL) rum and add ice until pitcher is 3/4 full. Top with club soda. Serve in cocktail glasses.

POMCOSMO

Combine 2 parts lemon vodka, 2 parts pomegranate juice and 1 part orange liqueur with crushed ice in a cocktail shaker. Shake and strain into a cocktail glass.

PIÑA COLADA MARTINI

Combine 1 part coconut rum, 3/4 part orange vodka and 2 parts pineapple juice with crushed ice in a cocktail shaker. Shake and strain into a cocktail glass. Drop in a cherry and add a drizzle of grenadine.

INDEX